# Collins
## LITTLE BOOKS

CW01024705

# BANANAGRAMS®
## SECRETS

HarperCollins Publishers
Westerhill Road
Bishopbriggs
Glasgow
G64 2QT

First Edition 2014
Reprinted with changes 2015, 2016
New Edition 2017

10 9 8 7 6 5 4 3 2 1 0

BANANAGRAMS® is the Registered
Trademark of Bananagrams, Inc. of
Providence, Rhode Island, U.S.A.
All Rights Reserved.
© 2017 Bananagrams, Inc.

ISBN 978-0-00-825046-1

www.harpercollins.co.uk

A catalogue record for this book is
available from the British Library

Author: Deej Johnson

Typeset by Davidson Publishing
Solutions

Printed and bound in China by
RR Donnelley APS Co Ltd

# Contents

# Foreword – Dame Judi Dench

I have always been a fan of word games, and BANANAGRAMS was first introduced to me by my daughter, Finty Williams. She was appearing at the Globe Theatre at the time and the whole company used to play the game ferociously every evening before going on stage. One night she brought home a banana-shaped bag and from that minute we were all hooked.

My addiction was instant; I loved the energy of the game, as well as the silliness of the banana pouch, and it soon became an essential companion. It has travelled with me to movie shoots all over the world, where I often cajole fellow cast and crew into games between takes!

Having been a BANANAGRAMS player for a while now, it is fair to say that my approach to the game has become a little routine. I have my own secret strategies for peeling and dumping – although I say "bunching" not "dumping" – but we can all do with polishing up our skills every once in a while! And that is exactly why I am so pleased to find that the people behind the game have chosen to share their marvellous wisdom, tricks and tips in this fascinating little book. Personally, I am looking forward to trying out some new tactics next time I play, as well as sampling some of the new game-play ideas the team have created. I hope you, too, enjoy discovering the sheer delight of BANANAGRAMS.

## About the Author

Writer, magician and anachronism Deej Johnson is a BANANAGRAMS fanatic, believing that the game perfectly blends fun, speed and language skills. He delights in finding new ways to get an edge while playing by the book… Deej serves as a creative consultant at BANANAGRAMS and claims that his former high-school teacher, Janise Marillat, summed him up best in an annual report that said: "His cheerful smile often gets him out of difficult situations… Unfortunately, these are usually situations that he creates himself."

## Good Eggs and Honest Bananas: How BANANAGRAMS Came To Be…

Abe Nathanson was a good egg and an honest banana! Now, the fact that 'honest banana' is an anagram of Abe Nathanson has absolutely nothing to do with the name BANANAGRAMS… But the game has everything to do with Abe's character, and three generations of his delightfully eccentric family who wanted to create a fast, fun diversion…

Despite some of the Nathansons living in the U.S. and some in the U.K., they were all united by 76-year-old Abe's love of wordplay, wit and fun: as a father, grandfather and friend, he was gently charismatic, effortlessly instilling his love of fun in others. Among those sharing his interests were his daughter – Rena – and Rena's children, Aaron, then ten, and Ava, then seven. Collectively, they conceived the notion of a new word game that would let people of all ages play anywhere, without endlessly waiting for turns... The idea soon began to develop: "What if it's a race? What if there's no board? What if you don't have to fiddle about with scores?"

As much joyful experimenting got underway, Rena's family returned to the U.K. and began testing letter combinations among friends... Abe continued working in Rhode Island, eventually telling people he had an anagram game that "drives people bananas!" In doing so, he stumbled on the name BANANAGRAMS! With the inherent silliness of bananas perfectly matching the game's spirit, the simple rules and lingo fell into place – and the obsession really began...

Many early players found it difficult to put away the distinctive banana-shaped pouches that Rena's mother Sandy made by hand, and in which the Nathansons gave away the game. Eventually, Rena arranged for a Rhode Island toy shop to stock BANANAGRAMS just to see if the idea of a commercial future for the game was to be... Or not to be! The answer was immediate: BANANAGRAMS flew off the shelf! This quiet success led to the game's official launch at the 2006 London Toy Fair.

Its popularity was instantaneous: the game quickly rose to the status of a modern classic, selling millions worldwide!

And while Abe sadly passed away in 2010, his love of family, play and fun live on. BANANAGRAMS is still run by co-inventor and Top Banana Rena. As a CEO, mother, boss and friend, Rena exudes the same spirit and values as her dad, and is just as appreciative of their good fortune, saying: "My thanks to everyone who supported our obsession in the early days! Thanks, too, to all those who continue to enjoy BANANAGRAMS. It's put us on an incredible journey – and we're having a great trip; thanks for joining us!" Of course, it helps that she's as mad as a bag of squirrels.

# BEFORE YOU BEGIN

# 'Monkeys Sip Teas'

That's not only a fun way to start a book, it's also an anagram of 'Some Sneaky Tips' – which is exactly what you'll find at the start of *The Little Book of BANANAGRAMS*! If you play BANANAGRAMS a lot, though, you already know that rearranging letters is only part of the game. You also have to be fast and strategic… And you have to know the rules! So here's a brief recap before we look at 'The Stinky Apes' – sorry, 'The Sneaky Tips'…

# Rules

Empty all 144 letters face-down on the table to form the **BUNCH**. Depending on the number of players, each person takes between 11 and 21 tiles. Up to four players may take the full 21; five – six players take 15 letters… Seven or more BANANAGRAMS fans each start with 11 tiles. In all cases, the game begins when a player shouts "**SPLIT**" and everyone turns over their tiles as fast as they humanly can! There's no taking turns – you simultaneously race to use your letters in an individual word grid, rearranging them as much as you like.

When you're out of letters, you shout "**PEEL**"… Everyone takes a new tile from the **BUNCH**, including the person who shouted "**PEEL**". If you get stuck with a difficult letter, you can say "**DUMP**" and return it – face-down – to the **BUNCH**… But you have to take three new letters in exchange! Once all the tiles in the **BUNCH** are used, the first player to legitimately use all their letters shouts "**BANANAS!**" and wins!

## Not Quite Rules

If you've ever heard the words "I'm sorry, I don't make the rules", you probably caught the subtext, "I just learn and quote them verbatim!" Well, with BANANAGRAMS, we really don't make all the rules. Some of them you have to decide for yourself… Nevertheless, here are our thoughts on the grey areas of the game!

## U.S. and U.K. Spellings

In the 1820s, Noah Webster radically reformed the American English language, changing dozens of the U.K.'s word spellings for a variety of reasons. And while his suggested spelling of machine – masheen – didn't find a home on either side of the Atlantic, many of his other changes survive to this day. In fact, the differences between British and American English now cause what we imagine to be about 80% of all word-game arguments!

If you plan to keep playing BANANAGRAMS with friends, though, you can avoid a debate by agreeing what's acceptable before you start. And while you could opt to play exclusively with U.S. or U.K. spellings, the strategically shrewd thing to do is to persuade others to allow both. This allows you to play many S's and Z's interchangeably, and for the letter U to slip in and out of words such as **COLOR**, **GLAMOR**, and **FLAVOR** as required! Of course, your opponents are able to do the same thing – the question is: will they think to do so?! See the section on U.S. / U.K. language for more Sneaky Tips…

# Abbreviations, Acronyms and Text Speak

A friend of ours was once told to remove – from a long, wordy report – "all the confusing **TLA**s". Unfortunately, no one had any idea what the boss meant by **TLA**s! When someone plucked up the nerve to ask, it turned out to mean 'Three Letter Abbreviations'! Well, most abbreviations, acronyms, and text speak are disallowed in BANANAGRAMS – unless they've come into common use as colloquialisms or shortened forms. For example, **AD** for advertisement is okay; **LOL** for 'Laugh Out

Loud' / 'Lots Of Love' is not. **AB** for an abdominal muscle is okay; **PLS** for 'please' is not. The best thing to do is remember the old speechwriters' adage: "If in doubt, leave it out".

# Defining Moments

The question of definitions often comes up in BANANAGRAMS when one player challenges another over a suspicious-looking word in their grid. If a word is clearly recognizable to other players, the decent thing to do is to allow it even if the person who used it isn't entirely sure what it means. That said, your intention should be to know the definition of words you're playing… And if you plan to use the obscure words in this book, you really should learn their meanings! Some of them look like absolute nonsense to the untrained eye.

In the spirit of good sportsmanship, though, we suggest that, even if a word no one knows ends up in a grid by mistake but – when checked – appears in a dictionary, you allow it. Rather than grumble when it happens to us, we simply make a note of the new word, its meaning – and the dictionary it's in – for future reference.

# Table Manners

One obscure thing that you might want to settle ahead of the game is whether or not players are allowing symbols that appear in the Periodic Table of Elements. Here at BANANAGRAMS HQ, we feel that doing so takes things a bit far. If you disagree, then it opens the game up to some truly terrific letter combos... But it's not for us – sorry!

With all this in mind, you'll find yourself ready to play on your own terms... But you'll find your actual game is much improved if you start using The Sneaky Tips at every stage of the game... It's not just about clever words. So – let's start at the beginning...

# Tile Turning I – Flipping Rows

You can get your grid off to a flying start when you know a few fast ways to turn tiles… This first way can be a little tricky to put over, so to help get to grips with the idea, physically take 21 tiles from the middle of the **BUNCH**. Arrange them in front of you in four rows of four tiles, and one row of five…

In other words, you have five neat rows of letters, all face-down, with the width of about two thumbs between each row, but with the tiles in each row touching. In a way, they look a bit like the rungs of a ladder! To turn them, you're going to make a shape that is reminiscent of someone eating a sandwich with both hands! Bring your hands together over the furthest row of tiles with your fingers on the far edges and your thumbs on the nearer edge…

If you look at the tiles, you should see that each of your thumb-tips is naturally positioned to touch two tiles simultaneously. So each thumb now pushes forwards at the same time and lifts its two tiles at the near edge, and rolls them over. The letters should drop onto their backs and scatter slightly at the same time.

Repeat this action on the next row of letters. Continue in this fashion, working towards yourself. When you reach the front row of five, make sure that the thumb on your dominant hand pinches and turns the three tiles. With practice, you might find you can do this maneuver with more tiles in each row – and fewer rows!

# Tile Turning II – Tile Piles

This alternative tile-turning strategy needs a little dexterity and occasionally causes controversy – but it gives you a few seconds' advantage right at the start of the game... At least until your opponent learns to do it as well!

To take 21 letters from the **BUNCH**, pinch one, face-down, somewhat from above, between the index and middle fingers and the thumb of your dominant hand. Now, counting that first tile as one, continue picking up four more tiles by bringing the pinched tile straight down on top of another face-down letter. As it moves around, your hand compensates for the erratic layout of the **BUNCH**, collecting a total of five tiles between the fingers in a move that looks reminiscent

of someone picking up poker chips! You end up with the five tiles stacked between
your fingers and thumbs. Use your other hand to straighten the pile, then deposit the letters – still face-down – right in front of you.

Repeat this stacking three more times but make sure you take six tiles on your last collection. When someone shouts "**SPLIT**", your dominant hand lifts up a stack and turns it sideways so that you're looking

at the tiles' edges. Your other hand takes the stack in a similar grip and smoothly spreads the tiles face-up on the table! It is a little bit of a knack, but this sounds trickier than it is. It's also worth mentioning that, on many

smooth surfaces, you might find that you can place a stack of letters down on their edges, with the tiles at a slight upward angle and cause them to spread pretty evenly just by letting go!

# Tile Turning III

Begin by collecting five tiles in the same way as for Tile Turning II. Place the stack down in front of you, but allow them to slope off each other in the direction of your dominant hand. The tiles should rest in a fashion that looks like a fallen 'domino chain'! In other words, the letters are all face-down but leaning on each other at an angle, with only one tile completely flat, and all the others with one edge resting on the table top.

Collect your next five letters and add them to the sloping pile in the same way. Continue making this long horizontal row of leaning tiles in front of you, until you have the full complement. When somebody shouts "**SPLIT**", it's a simple matter to pivot the first tile over using your weaker hand, tipping it face-up so that all of the other letters flip over too. If your dominant hand helps guide the tiles from above, the whole maneuver takes as little as three seconds!

As the tiles turn, spread them with your fingers while simultaneously searching for helpful letters.

# More Tile Turning...

If your hands are somewhat on the large side, you have a tile-turning advantage! You're more likely to be able to use the next two techniques without sending piles of tiles scattering to the four corners of the room.

# Tile Turning IV

In much the same way as you turn tiles in Tile Turning III, stack your initial selection in piles. Here, though, one pile should have 11 tiles, the other just 10. To lift them, bring your dominant hand over the nearer stack and lower it so that your middle finger and thumb reach down the sides to grip the bottom tile. Meanwhile, your index finger curls up in such a way that it can rest on the top-most tile, and apply a little pressure...

Be careful! You don't want to apply so much pressure that you send the middle letters shooting out, but nor do you want to apply so little that they fall on the table before you need them to. When someone says "**SPLIT**", lift and simultaneously turn the stack so that you can place it between the index finger and thumb of your other hand. Now, when you go to put your tiles down, tilt them slightly so that they're more face-up, and place them somewhat on their edges. They'll automatically slip apart and spread out on the table. Don't bother to check that they're doing that, though: instead just quickly pick up the second stack and repeat the move.

# Tile Turning V

If ever there has been a holy grail of tile turning, it's a method by which, somehow, one would be able to have all 21 tiles ready to go, hear the word "**SPLIT**", then pick up, turn, release and spread all of the tiles in one go. Well, happily, some people can now do just that. Here's how…

Stack two sets of ten tiles side by side. The two piles must be absolutely straight, square and touching all the way up. If necessary, use a notebook or two credit cards, etc., as a sort of squaring tool to ensure they're completely true. Next put the last tile – number 21 – on top of both stacks. In other words, the final tile is half on the left pile, half on the right, bridging them. Now put your dominant hand in a position directly comparable to that used in Tile Turning IV… The only difference is that instead of the middle finger and thumb holding just the bottom tile, they now grip both bottom tiles at the point where they touch.

Meanwhile, the curled index finger applies pressure, just as before, by gently pushing down on the top-most tile. In this way the two stacks are effectively clamped together. On "**SPLIT**" you lift them as if they're one unit. Transfer all of the tiles to your other hand, now clamping the two stacks together between the fingers and thumb. This is why it's so important to make sure that the stacks are truly square. If they're not, they'll split apart during the transfer and fall higgledy-piggledy. Assuming that you've done it correctly, though, move your dominant hand completely out of the way, and don't worry if the top-most tile now falls to the table; the rest won't be far behind…

Keeping the other fingers of your submissive hand out of the way, place all the tiles clamped between the index finger and thumb down on the table surface. Put them somewhat on their sides. Provided the surface is smooth enough, they'll begin splaying out and spreading all on their own.

# All Fingers and Thumbs

Years ago, a 'finger' was a formal unit of measurement equivalent to three quarters of an inch – almost exactly the width of a BANANAGRAMS tile. Believe it or not, though, the tiles are a full inch wide on the diagonal – about the same as some people's thumbs! How does that help? Well, it means that when you're playing Tile Turning V, you can twist the top-most tile 45 degrees askew… That gives you an extra quarter of an inch's width to act as a clamp.

# Jumble Your Letters

When you use the tile-turning techniques, you should find the letters land in a bit of a jumble rather than a neat row. That's great! But even if you turn tiles in a more conventional way, make sure you leave them in a face-up mishmash rather than a straight line. When letters are laid out in a line, most people tend to consider only the first few – and miss opportunities to start in style. On no account should you begin by arranging your tiles – as one new player did – in alphabetical order!

# Clusters

Some people find it helps to spend time clustering letters together in 'likely combinations' – for example, **C**'s with **K**'s – after they initially turn over their tiles. While this sometimes pays off with the difficult letters, it's often something of a false economy. Once they're face-up, don't spend time fussing with letters: focus on your Opening Gambit instead.

# Law of the Jumble

There's a terrific piece of text online that tells how a piece of research suggests that "It ofetn deosn't mttaer in waht oredr the ltteers in a wrod are… If the frist and lsat ltteers are in the rghit pclae, you can sitll raed the othres bcuseae yuor mnid raeds wrdos as a whole."*

Weird, isn't it? And while we have a fair few questions about the value and origin of this, the idea itself leads us to a similar point. Generally speaking, players are able to look at a jumble of random letters and intuitively find at least a few decent words lurking in the chaos. The following approaches help you play that all-important first word; they're the techniques that a lot of fast players use…

*We can't find who wrote the original – and this isn't it, but it's simialr. Sorry – similar.

# The Opening Gambit

Did you know that the word **GAMBIT** originates from the Latin for leg – gamba – via Italian, gambetto? It literally means 'a tripping up', which is why it has the connotation of a move designed to wrong-foot others. Even if you regularly play BANANAGRAMS with friends, you may not think of it as a game of wrong-footing strategy! And yet you can significantly boost your chances of winning when you choose to make an opening move that preferably uses no fewer than four, but ideally six or more tiles.

# Straight Flush

'The Opening Gambit' – playing six letters or more in your first or second word – gives you more playing options for the entire game. It becomes especially effective if the word you play also clears out some of the more difficult letters. J, Q, V, X, and Z are widely considered the hardest to play, so – if you have them – flush some out straight away and leave yourself with more flexible letters for follow-up words. You'd be amazed at how many people don't do this, and start playing words with their easy letters… They almost immediately find themselves left with all the work-shy minions of the alphabet! Try to put the harder-to-use letters in the *middle* of those words, too. We'll look into this later.

## One Down, Two Across

There's an old gag, beloved by wordsmiths, that involves feigning a struggle to remember who it was that invented the modern crossword puzzle: "Arthur somebody!" they say, adding, "I can't recall his surname but it's five letters; **W**, **Y**, something, something, **E**…" Hey – we said it was old, not good! In any case, the crossword-like phrase 'one down, two across' is at the heart of another Sneaky Tip that often saves vital seconds if you play BANANAGRAMS regularly…

It seems that most players find it slightly easier to envision horizontal words. For that reason they tend to start with one. If they're playing a step format, they then have to work a little harder to find two vertical words. But if you play your first word vertically, you make the next two words in your grid a little easier! And if you're using a tile-turning technique, along with the **'IS NEAT'** concept* or another statistically probable word, you can imagine how the various slight speed advantages hurry you on towards a win. Ah! It was Wynne! Arthur Wynne invented the modern crossword…

*We'll explain this soon!

# Get an Edge at the Edge

If you've ever heard something chaotic described as "a shambles" and wondered where on earth such a word came from, excellent news... We're going to tell you! Years ago, a shambles was a table or bench used by butchers to display pieces of meat. Later, it's thought a limb-strewn and bloodied battlefield was said to look like a shambles – and that word eventually came to represent any kind of disarray. Charming story! In any case, if you've ever tried to move a grid that's been built too close to the edge of a table then perhaps you already know a little bit about disarray... Here are three tips to help you avoid such a shambles.

# Begin with the End in Mind

The table's edge is one of the very few known factors in a hand of BANANAGRAMS. That's why some switched-on players place a long word parallel to the bottom edge right at the start of the game, marrying this strategy with One Down, Two Across. The word should be no more than two tiles' height away from the actual edge. This leaves enough space to play letters in the way shown on the next page. That means that you can still get underway using most of the advice about 'The Opening Gambit', 'One Down,

Two Across' and 'Steps' – but it also establishes the grid's lower edge early, allows you to place some two- and three-letter words down at great speed, and gives you lots of space to build upwards.

# Fluster. Restful.

Odd that the letters in the word **FLUSTER** anagram into a word associated with an opposite state: **RESTFUL**… Some wordsmiths call that an 'antigram'. In any case, the opposite approach to starting very close to the edge is, of course, to begin building your grid much further in on the table and simply accept that, at some point, you're going to run out of room lower down. You just have to have a definite cut-off point: don't make the mistakes of balancing tiles on the table's edge, 'bending' words to make one more letter fit in, or starting an entirely separate grid in the hope that others will forgive you! They won't.

# Build into the Bunch

Imagine you have two buckets of water. In Bucket A, the water has a temperature of 40 degrees Fahrenheit; the water in Bucket B has a temperature of 32 degrees Fahrenheit. If you drop a BANANAGRAMS tile in both, from the same height at the same time, which tile sinks faster? This quirky question reminds us not to overlook obvious answers… The tile you drop in Bucket A would sink considerably faster: if the water in Bucket B has a temperature of 32 degrees Fahrenheit, then it's actually frozen solid. A tile would only sink when the firm ice thawed – could be hours!

Sometimes working out where to build parts of your grid is a little like the ice question… It's obvious, but it's easy for some to overlook: where you envision the top of your grid being is often restricted only by the tiles in the **BUNCH**. But, in fact, the **BUNCH** continually shrinks! In other words, if you start playing well away from the edge of your table, then extend your grid both upwards and downwards as required, there's a really good chance that the **BUNCH** won't be in the way by the time you get up there! That said, even if it is, there's nothing to stop you placing some tiles in a way that encroaches on the **BUNCH**: just shove the face-down tiles out of the way – better this than falling off that table edge!

# Let Words Pop

As soon as you can, just glance at your letters. Does a word of five, six or seven letters just pop out at you? With experience you'll start seeing words in the muddle more and more easily. After a while, you won't need to think too much about your first move – you'll be going straight in to The Opening Gambit. Meanwhile...

# Look for Patterns

The letters that spell either **IS NEAT**, **RATIONED**, **SATIRES** or **RETINAS** are among the patterns for which we first look. Later, we'll explain how these tiles can start you building your grid quickly and helpfully. For now, though, let's talk about putting the letters down strategically...

# Tile Positioning

The positioning of each and every tile in your grid dictates, to some degree, what your options are going to be later. To put that in a so-called 'aptogram': Positioning – Is Optioning! So in a moment we'll explain the 'Steps' system – a playing strategy that we think gives you the most positioning options most often. First, though, here's why tile positioning is vital at every stage.

## Here, SPOT

Take a look the first picture below. It shows a couple of words you're building at the start of a grid, and the letters **S**, **P** and **O** that still need putting in that area. You may well spot an obvious place to set them down quickly: above the word **SHOUT**, you could easily put them there and make the word **SPOT**! Then what? Do you see how cramped that option leaves your grid? The bottom two pictures show far more open grid structures. Realistically, they allow up to half as many options again as the second picture. This basic layout is what we refer to as a 'Step' – the key to avoiding **GRIDLOCK**...

# Gridlock

While it feels like an old and familiar word, **GRIDLOCK** is something of an infant, first appearing during New York City's 'Great Transit Strike' – in 1980! Referring to the fear that traffic could lock up and affect the New York grid system, a city traffic report suggested officials would "...participate in a grid lock prevention program." **GRIDLOCK** – as one word – swiftly came to mean any situation in which nothing can move. It perfectly describes the BANANAGRAMS scenario in which one plays hastily made words too closely together and squashes up the word grid to the point of impasse! Here's how to avoid it...

# Play 'Steps'

So first, have plenty of space around your intended grid in every direction. Play your first word vertically, making sure it's a longer one and that you then concentrate your attention on building 'outwards' in opposite directions near the ends. Go for words of four to six letters if you can; your grid should quickly start to resemble a rickety staircase! When you use this 'step approach', keep in mind that the letters you play near the beginning and end of one word will often become letters near the beginning and end of others...

# So it Begins...

As an example, imagine vertically playing the
letters in **QUINCE** as a first word. You have a
**C** and an **E** down the bottom with which you
can construct the end of a new word. That's not
too bad! But at the top, you want to hurriedly
produce at least a three-letter word that begins
with a **Q** or a **U**... Not ideal! Between them, **Q**
and **U** are estimated to be the first letters in just
over 3% of English words.

Q
U
I
N
C
E

If, though, you use the exact same letters to
spell **CINQUE**, you position the **U** and **E** near
the end of the word that will step to the left
– still not too bad! But instead of a **Q** or **U**
starting the word that will extend to the right,
you have a **C** or an **I**. **C** and **I** are estimated
to begin nearly 14% of English words. So all
things being equal, that simple change of order gives
you four times as many options! Get into the habit of
building words in this more discriminating way.

C
I
N
Q
U
E

# Common First and Last Letters

In regard to statistics, there are some wildly differing
lists purporting to determine the commonality of first
and last letters. As a rule of thumb, though, you might

want to consider **CAT PaDS** as a mnemonic to recall the letters that commonly start words.* Research also suggests that more than half of all words end with **E**, **T**, **D** and **S**, with **N** coming next. So think **END SeT**!

# Blind Spot

Rather than starting to obsess about what research says, though, pay attention to the letters with which you personally have blind spots. For example, one of the BANANAGRAMS team has great and inexplicable difficulty playing the letter **C**! We won't say which of the team because it wouldn't be fair on Deej… In any case, make time to learn a few more words that start or end with your blind-spot letters, or structure your game so that they more often appear in the middle of words.

# Housekeeping

Later on in your hand, it gets harder to maintain a Steps layout as the emphasis of the game shifts more towards getting rid of each new letter as quickly as possible. But speed isn't everything… To illustrate this, imagine that the top picture on the next page shows part of a grid that, perhaps out of necessity, is being built a little too quickly. It's starting to lose its

*The letters given are not in their correct order – just a memorable one!

'Step' structure... Now, for anyone who knows their two- and three-letter words, the obvious place to put the **T** that's just been peeled is next to the **A** in **KA**, to make **KAT**. Is that effective, though? See, while it gets rid of the T quickly enough, there's a good chance that playing **KAT** not only shuts off that horizontal line but also blocks the downward extension of **O** words from **ADO**...

# Nip and Tuck

So rather than playing the fast option – **KAT** – or taking tricky letters and just putting them on key words, some players would prefer to take a few seconds to nip and tuck that area of the grid. For example, it might be that the **A** of **KA** moves under the **T** of **TAR** to help make **TAT**. Alternatively, the other picture shows another way to place the **A** and the **T**, putting them both nearer the top of the grid. These Nip and Tuck actions might take fractionally longer than a straight placement, but they're preferable to playing **KAT**.

35

# Middles

You'll need to know a little about phonetics, music scales, reckless ambition and lacework to make complete sense of this... But imagine making an **S** into the word **ES**. **ES** becomes **TES**, **TES** turns to **ATES**, then **TATES** and **STATES**, which grows to **ESTATES**, then **RESTATES** and – finally – **PRESTATES**!

This unlikely wordplay illustrates the kind of backward thinking that comes in handy when one builds off the middle letters of words... How so? Well, while it initially helps to think of your BANANAGRAMS word grid as an uneven staircase, you will – at some point – want to make better use of the letters in the middle of words, too. Wherever possible, use middle letters to:

- Branch out and make new steps in opposite directions to the nearest step
- Quickly play difficult tiles in short words
- Create words that babysit vowels and **S**'s, etc.

# Which Way's Up?

**NOON.** Lovely word; beautiful palindrome!* At just four letters, it's the longest in English that, when typed in capital letters, reads the same backwards as forwards and upside down! The capital letters that have no wrong way up in the alphabet are **H, I, N, O, S, X** and **Z**... But here at BANANAGRAMS HQ, we don't particularly worry about any of that! Fussing to make sure your letters are the right way up eats away quite a bit of time... If you can read your grid when the letters are facing every which way, play them like that.

# Dumping: For and Against

BANANAGRAMS moves at a terrific pace and it's infuriating to lose your momentum because you pick up a tricky letter. As you play the game more and more, you might begin to wonder if dumping is a false economy! Generally speaking, we think dumping pays off better in the early stages of a game and really helps beginners who have yet to develop more strategies.

---

*Most people know a few palindromes – that's to say words that read the same backwards as forwards... We're really excited by palindrome phrases, though and – missing apostrophe aside – this is a doozy: **MARGE LETS NORAH SEE SHARONS TELEGRAM!**

# When NOT to Dump

The more you and other players call "**DUMP**" during a game, the greater the chances that you'll pick up difficult letters toward the end. Think about it: none of you are likely to be putting back a lot of vowels, are you? So, as a general rule, the later it is in the game, the more risky it is to "**DUMP**".

# When TO Dump

Here's an interesting dumping strategy you might try early on when the **BUNCH** still has an abundance of decent tiles. If you have an inordinate number of difficult letters and are desperate, **DUMP** them all! Yes, it's a little risky as you end up with far more tiles… Remember, though, you ideally want a couple of longer words near the beginning to give your grid a solid core, so if there is a time to be bold, it's in the first few moves.

# When Else TO Dump

Another time at which it can help to **DUMP** is when you can see at a glance that you're only one letter away from being able to play a Pattern Technique. If that's the case, and you also have a few tricky letters, you can sometimes "**DUMP**" in the hope that you'll pick up the required tile. Don't fall into the trap of repeatedly dumping in search of an elusive pattern component, though. We'll explain the Pattern Techniques shortly.

# New Tiles for Old

It should be fairly apparent that, when you pick up a harder-to-play letter, you can always look for ways to quickly switch it for an easier one in your grid. For example if you pick up a **B** and have already played **LUNCH** – and the **L** is free from intersection – changing **LUNCH** to **BUNCH** probably helps increase your chances of moving forward swiftly: **L** is estimated to appear in nearly three times more words than **B**. This basic principle lies behind the next approach, which takes it up a gear.

# Dumping in Your Grid

Sky walker. Funambulist. Equilibrist. Three terms you might want to consider instead of the rather mundane 'tightrope walker' should it ever come up! And come up it does when we discuss the art of dumping difficult letters in your own grid. That's because this technique is a little bit like walking a tightrope: one wrong move and it could finish you off! The idea is this: if you've picked up a difficult letter, and the temptation is to **DUMP** it immediately, take a quick look at your grid first. Ask yourself: is there somewhere this tile could go if, instead of thinking of ways to add it to your grid, you instead think of it as an exchange for a few other letters? The top picture shows a great example: neither the word **CHASES** nor the word **CODED** lets you get rid of a freshly-peeled **Q**...

Rather than **DUMP** it, though, you could break the end off **CODED**, and put the **Q** on **C** & **O** to make **COQ**. That means you now have a **D**, **E** and **D** to get rid of – and there are at least three ways to do that with hardly any effort. The advantage of this is that you aren't returning a tile that could be much harder to get rid of later if you're planning to use the techniques we'll discuss in 'Rapid Peeling'. It also eliminates chance: you don't know which three letters you'd get in a straight **DUMP** – but you know exactly what you're going to get by dumping

in your grid. Finally, keep in mind that while you don't have to take three tiles from your grid, you certainly shouldn't take many more: you don't want to restructure everything.

# Dirty Dumping I

Have you ever dumped a tile only to pick it up again a few peels later? There are two strategies for avoiding this. First, when you **DUMP** a tile, place it back at the outside edge of the **BUNCH**. But when you pick up your letters, take them from the middle...

# Dirty Dumping II

This is a somewhat underhand – but entirely 'legal' – dumping tactic. Return your difficult letters to the **BUNCH** by openly placing them immediately in front of an adjacent opponent. There's a good chance they won't be paying attention to you. However, be warned... While this isn't against the rules, it might turn a game with friends into a game with former friends if they catch on!

# Dirty Dumping III

Use the hand that deposits the unwanted tile to help conceal the exact point at which you return it to the **BUNCH**. If you place tiles back openly, it increases the chance that eagle-eyed opponents will see where you're putting them – and avoid them!

# Dirty Dumping IV

The saying "What's good for the goose is good for the gander" sums up our attitude towards this fast method of picking up three new letters immediately after you **DUMP** a tile. Put your undesirable letter back, then use the poker-chip maneuver from Tile Turning **II** to pick up the replacements in one swift action. As your hand comes towards your tile area, turn them face-up. Without hesitating, take the tiles between the fingers of your other hand, spreading them as you put them down.

# Dump Fan

If your new letters look easy to place, you may prefer not to put them down at all. Some people use the fingers and thumbs of each hand to fan out the three new tiles. With two letters in the dominant hand and one in the weaker, you might find you can pop the new tiles straight into words and save the time involved in putting them down and picking them up again.

## Cheeky PEEL

How many times do you call "**PEEL**" and pick up a tile when you play BANANAGRAMS? "A lot!" is a good enough answer, since it depends on your skill, and the number of players you're facing. But what if, every time you did it, you could give yourself a tiny advantage? Well... It won't win you any friends if people realize what you're doing but you can try this: instead of saying "**PEEL**" immediately after you've placed the last letter in your grid, start saying it just before your hand picks up the new tile from the **BUNCH**. That way you already have a letter in hand at the point when everyone else is reaching for a new one.

## PEEL! PEEL! PEEL!

Ever been playing BANANAGRAMS and had a despairing or ill-at-ease feeling because one person calls "**PEEL!**" "**PEEL!**" "**PEEL!**" so quickly? Well, while those rapid-repeat cries can be discouraging, keep in mind that players saying it over and over again in quick succession are very likely creating a lot of two-

or three-letter words without an overall strategy. That means they're more likely to have a major rework on their hands – or a jarring **DUMP** – when they pick up a tricky letter.

# The 'S' Instinct Part I

As soon as you begin to make regular time to play BANANAGRAMS, you may want to try a few ways of getting better in the long run. This is a great strategy: start developing your awareness of gratuitous pluralizing, and the habit of adding **S**'s to verbs! If you can cultivate a feeling for where, in your word grid, you can effortlessly spirit away a spare **S**, you're ahead of the game – or games… Keep this in mind when you read the section on 'Statistically Likely Words'.

# The 'S' Instinct Part II

Just as it's helpful to develop the **S** instinct to get rid of **S**'s quickly, it's almost as handy for getting them back! Having added unnecessary **S**'s to words, you'll automatically be in a better position to pull some of them back when you need to play them where an **S** is essential.

# Keep an Eye on Dictionaries

"I was reading the dictionary. I thought it was a poem about everything…" So says comedian Steven Wright! We love the idea and it ties in with the advantage you can gain in any word game by being attentive to changes in dictionaries. They often fold in new words: sometimes these updates make the press, sometimes not. For obvious reasons, online dictionaries are usually first to venture forth with words such as **SELFIE** and **RETWEET**… Peel your eyes for revisions to leading dictionaries, and focus particular attention on short words.

# Which Dictionary?

We talk more about how words become words in different dictionaries in The Bit at the Back of the Book… For now, the question as to which dictionary to use is best answered by saying, "Lots of them!" No one dictionary contains every word about which we talk in *The Little Book of BANANAGRAMS*. For some, part of the fun comes from trying to persuade people that, say, **CHERT** is a type of sedimentary rock or what have you. That said, there's absolutely nothing to stop you pulling out this book and pointing to the definitions in here. The only word of warning we give is to be mindful of user-generated content online: you may never hear the end of it if you point an indicatory finger at a nonsense definition online.[*]

# Gird Your Grid

More often than not you can find the word **CLEW** in dictionaries meaning a particular part of a ship's sail. Originally, however, a **CLEW** was a ball of yarn. Indeed, it was just such a ball of yarn that Theseus supposedly trailed behind him to escape the Minotaur's Labyrinth in Greek mythology. And did you guess? It's from this definition of **CLEW** that we get the modern word **CLUE**.

The trouble when you first start to play BANANAGRAMS is that the grids you build are a bit like the labyrinth when you haven't got a clew. You don't know which letters are coming next and you can't know how the grid's going to come together – so it's enormously difficult to know which strategy to use, or when…

That's why having the option to break up and rebuild your grid appears valuable. You can scrap everything and start all over again if you want to. Be warned: that's a very dangerous way to play! Indeed, most players with experience avoid making radical changes

[*]It might amuse you to know indicatory is an anagram of dictionary.

at all costs. If it's completely unavoidable, however, there are a few sneaky tips that can make it easier. Let's start with a common mistake though...

# Don't Slide on a PEEL...

Many people waste up to two seconds every single time they say **"PEEL"**. That's because when they take a tile, they slide it closer towards themselves before looking at it. It's almost as if they're playing cards and don't want people to see what they have! Only when it's right in front of them do they then turn their tile over. If you've been doing that, break the habit. Instead, look at the letter immediately after you pick it up. Register what you have, then look straight back down at your grid to start working out where it can go. Again, it only gives you a tiny advantage – but if you use this approach alongside 'Cheeky Peel', the tiny advantages really start add up!

# Sliding Words

While it's a great idea to pick up individual tiles as you take them from the **BUNCH**, it's a painfully inefficient method for transplanting a larger section of grid. You need to move letters you've already played with much greater efficiency. One way to do that with a word of up to four letters is to put one fingertip on top of each tile, press down on them just a little, then slide them wherever they need to go. By the way, this tip and the following techniques presume you're playing on a smooth surface with only a little grip such as a tablecloth, etc.

# 6/11

To move a larger number of tiles – some say as many as 11, but one has to imagine that these people have hands big enough to palm a couple of melons – try this… Make – say – a vertical six-letter word. Now extend your index finger and rest the tip of it on the tile furthest from you. The others run down the length of your finger and, depending on the size of your hands, end somewhere around the base of that finger or the ball of your thumb. Exert a little downward pressure and move the whole word.

# 6/11+

If you play your grid neatly, you might find you can shift T-shaped letter groups using the 6/11 move. Your index finger can lie atop a vertical column of tiles while the balls of your other fingers rest on a horizontal row. It's a fast and fairly safe way of moving between six to eleven tiles going in one direction and four to six going the other. Remember, too, that you can turn your whole hand to move horizontal letters.

# Wer die Wahl hat, hat die Qual

Roughly translated this German proverb means, 'He who has a choice has the doldrums'. There's no time to muck about in BANANAGRAMS, so when you find a technique that works for you, stop making choices! Most people's middle finger is the longest, for example, but some can't use it for the 6/11 technique on account that they find it harder to lift all the other fingers out of the way. Experiment, but focus on what you think has the most impact in the shortest time.

# Chunks of Grid

We've already cautioned you against moving large parts of your grid and must do so again! You might find, however, that you can move as many as 12 to 15 tiles, perhaps more, by simply lowering your whole hand onto a group of letters, applying a slight pressure and sliding them en masse. There's a good chance that some tiles will cling to your hand, though, so this technique is best used sparingly. We only risk it when we're desperate to shift words along a few tiles' widths.

# BANANAGRAMS Variations!

If you plan on playing BANANAGRAMS a lot, you may find that you want to practice some strategies and word lists by squeezing games in here and there as time permits. Here are some variations of BANANAGRAMS for a number of situations! The first four are solitaire versions; you can play them at leisure or against the clock. We've suggested time limits for some of them, but feel free to adjust as your game improves!

## One Player Games

**Bananalone**
**ALONE** means solitary. Take away the A from **ALONE** and you're left with **LONE** – which means solitary... Now take away the L from **LONE**: you're left with **ONE**, which – you get the idea! To play Bananalone, put all the tiles face-down and take 21 of them for yourself. Play BANANAGRAMS as usual, but only **PEEL** once your original letters are gone. Keep going, and see how long it takes to use up all 144 tiles. Keep trying to beat your best time by using some of the Sneaky Tips and word lists in this book.

## Bananalonger

A very challenging variation of Bananalone involves playing the game as described, but using as few words as possible. You must still use all 144 letters and stick to the rules – just make longer words at a more casual pace.

## Tough Bananas

Randomly take any ten letters from the pouch and place them face-down on the table... Next, remove ten more face-up, and mix them in with those on the table so you end up with 20 tiles in a face-up, face-down mishmash! Now create a word grid as quickly as you can, using only the face-up tiles! Once they've gone, turn over the remaining letters and work those into your grid. You can set yourself a time limit of one minute for this game. With no peeling or dumping, there's a definite possibility that you may find it impossible to move at all – but that's why we call the game Tough Bananas!

## Bangram

If you're short of time and space, but you really want to play BANANAGRAMS, this condensed version is for you. Take 25 letters from the pouch and put them face-down in front of you. Set a clock on your phone or tablet for a one-and-a-half-minute countdown.

You can time it with a watch if you'd rather, but looking at your wrist wastes valuable time! Start the countdown, turn over the tiles, and begin to make the word grid as fast as you can. You're not allowed to **PEEL**... You're not allowed to **DUMP**! Ninety seconds is a very tight time-frame, but see if you can beat the clock using all 25 tiles.

# For Two or More Players

### Banana Smoothie
Looking for something less frantic? Equally divide all the tiles, face-down, among the players. After you say "**SPLIT**", you turn your tiles face-up. Now the usual rules apply but, instead of peeling and dumping, you use only the letters you took. The first player to use up all their letters says "**BANANAS!**" and wins!

### Best Banana
Each player takes 15 tiles... Then, instead of making a grid, each player has to make the longest word they can using their letters. Give points for the longest word. You could instead make this a contest to spell the most words, find the most unusual words, or even the best all-round words... Though judging 'the best' could be – erm – controversial, perhaps!

## Banana Café

Those who take advantage of the portability of BANANAGRAMS – let's call it its Bananagramobility – may enjoy this variation, which is shorter and takes up less space, making it ideal for playing in cafés, restaurants, and the like. With the BANANAGRAMS pouch full of tiles on the table, each player takes 21 letters and plays as normal. However, while you can still **DUMP**, no one is allowed to **PEEL**. The first player to use up all of their letters says "**BANANAS!**" and wins.

## Paper Bananas

Play BANANAGRAMS as normal, but limiting the area of the word grids. Begin with a standard-size sheet of paper as a playing area… In other words, you're not allowed to extend your grid off the paper! This makes BANANAGRAMS more challenging as you work harder to find words that fit. If you have a lot of players – or are feeling particularly brave – try making the paper smaller!

## Banana Themes

If you play BANANAGRAMS as a regular group, you can enjoy the game in the usual way with one twist: players' grids must include one or more words related to a given theme. The more words you agree to include, the harder the game becomes. Ideas for themes are limited only by your imagination, but our list includes names of family members and friends, famous people, objects in the room, countries and capital cities, animals, sports, clothes, weather, parts of the body, TV shows, and films or books...

## Banana Count

This variation sees people playing BANANAGRAMS but with agreed restrictions: you must either form a specific number of words, or you must make words of a specified length. For example, you might agree that each player's grid will contain only four words, or that they can only use five-letter words. The fewer words allowed, or the longer the words specified, the tougher the game becomes.

## Bluff Bananas

This is a terrific game for glottologists, logophiles and philologists... Word lovers, let's call them! You'll need to prepare for it but, essentially, you play BANANAGRAMS in the usual way. After the game is over, each player takes the necessary letters to seemingly create three really obscure words... One of these you should have found in advance, the other two you invent completely! Now you give definitions for all three words. The real one is given truthfully whilst you fabricate definitions for the other two. Your opponents do the same, with the object being for each player to determine which words are true and which are pure bluff. No points given – just kudos for presenting the false words in a seemingly equident fashion*.

## Take Two
Looking for a slightly shorter version of the game? Set yourself up to play BANANAGRAMS in the usual way. When the time comes to **PEEL**, however, instead of taking one tile, each player takes two. As well as making the game a little shorter in duration, you may also find it causes a more subtle change... Double peeling sometimes reduces the number of obscure two-letter words that people use, which in turn evens out the game a little when there are different skill levels at the table.

## Bananart of Lying
Leaving 10 unidentified tiles in the pouch, you play BANANAGRAMS as usual... The twist is that – throughout the game – you may play up to five tiles in your grid face-down. These may or may not be the correct letters to complete the words in which

---

*Equident, defined as 'Fair of tooth': derived from the Latin aequi, meaning equal; and dent – French for tooth. Sometimes erroneously connected with the origins of the Tooth Fairy, equident is actually said of those whom one could trust in much the same way that 'langue fourchue' or 'forked tongue' was ascribed to those you could not... This is what equident means! Or did we make it up?

they sit... When someone shouts **"BANANAS!"** the other players check the word grid for errors, then ask how many of the face-down tiles are incorrect. The player under scrutiny chooses either to answer truthfully, or to lie. They could have one false spelling and claim that they have two; they may have none and say four... Or have none and say none! In any case, the other players now have to decide whether or not the would-be winner is lying or telling the truth. They must agree and give a verdict. If the 'winner' is caught in a lie, they lose! The penalty imposed on a false accusation of lying varies but usually involves drinking... But drinking responsibly, obviously!

**Bacon 'n' Bananas**
The entire **BUNCH** is face-up on the table. Each player thinks of two disparate but very famous movie stars... Jotting them down on a piece of paper, everyone passes these names to the player on their left. Someone yells **"ACTION!"** and you all look at your names, then race to build a grid of movie star names that link the two in a BANANAGRAMS / Six Degrees of Separation mash up! If you think you've succeeded, you shout **"BACON"**, in honor of seemingly omnipresent actor Kevin Bacon! You must explain your grid in the same way you would when playing Six Degrees of Kevin Bacon.

## BANANAGRAMS Pairs

Take out two sets of complete alphabet letters A–Z. Turn them face-down and mix all 52 tiles into one **BUNCH**. Be thorough! Now, openly turn over any two tiles… If they match – and the chances are that they won't – pick up the pair! That person now takes another turn and continues to play until they fail to find a pair. The aim of the game is to be the first to collect three pairs of identical letters. The list of variations of this game includes matching different numbers of letters – five pairs, ten or all 26 – as well as finding only the vowels, etc.

The memory-testing nature of this game also makes it ideal for a solo version. Meanwhile, just about every parent and teacher can recognize the potential educational value of word and letter-based games… You can use BANANAGRAMS tiles in numerous ways to teach children phonics, the alphabet and letter recognition, as well as help improve their spelling, vocabulary, grammar and – for younger children – making memory play more fun. For that age especially, you may find that, after shuffling the tiles, it helps to arrange them in neat rows rather than a mishmash. Keep the game fairly short, too. It makes sense to use BANANAGRAMS as one of a few games that you play to aid language skills.

## After Bananas

Almost any game in which you use BANANAGRAMS tiles can be educational at the end – but still fun! You might try naming a letter and having a child hand it to you. You can then place it down in front of you before asking for another letter, then another, etc. When you have the letters you want, ask the child to rearrange them into the order of choice!

So it might be that you ask for letters that help with any spelling homework that they have, or all 26 letters to arrange in alphabetical order. Speaking of which, there's no real reason to notice that the description of this game started with the word **ALMOST**... Lots of people believe it to be the longest English word in which all the letters appear only once and in alphabetical order! Well, it almost is – but not quite. There's a genus of grass that beats it by two letters: **AEGILOPS** – also known, rather charmingly, as goat's grass.

## Banattleships

A rather curious use of BANANAGRAMS tiles sees them form a five-by-five grid to play a compact version of the old pen and paper game Battleships! Each player takes the following tiles: **A** × 3, **C** × 1, **D** × 2, **E** × 4.

Then, one player helps themselves to 9 × **T** with 6 × **I**, while the other takes 9 × **R** and the remaining 6 × **I**'s.

Using a book or some such to screen their tiles, each player arranges the letters as if they were vessels in a fleet! Try not to worry too much about scale or historical accuracy and think of them like this: the **C** represents a Cruiser; a **C** is made with one line and there's one tile! The Destroyers are the **D**'s – made with two lines and two tiles. The **A** represents part of an Aircraft Carrier; there are three strokes in the letter and three of them. Finally, the **E** is for E-Boat and, because there are four lines in an **E**, there are four **E** tiles in this game...

So informed, each player turns all their tiles face-down and conceals their respective fleet among the various **I**'s, **R**'s and **T**'s in a five-by-five square. Obviously, the two **D** tiles must go next to each other and so on; the **I**'s, **R**'s and **T**'s serve as 'misses'. When you're both ready, one player removes the screen and points to a tile in the opponent's square. This letter is turned over... If it's a 'hit', the tile is left in place; if it's a 'miss' the **I**, **R** or **T** is removed and placed to one side. The other player then takes a turn and this continues until one of the players' entire fleet is exposed!

### The Big BANGANAGRAMS Theory

Many dictionaries define the word **GEEK** as a boring, unattractive social misfit, suggesting that it originates from the nineteenth-century Scottish **GECK**, meaning fool! Only more recently has it taken on the meaning of an obsessive and, in particular, a person with advanced computer, technical, or scientific knowledge. Go us! Is it not written that the geek shall inherit the Earth? Well, no, it isn't, but maybe there was a typo. Nevertheless, this game tasks card-carrying, badge-wearing nerds to try this with BANANAGRAMS tiles…

Take out the J's and Q's. Turn the other letters face-down and mix them thoroughly; divide the tiles equally among players and turn them face-up. You must now race to use as many tiles as possible while making words that can only be spelled with the table of elements. That is to say words like **C Ho Co La Te**, **Ba Co N**, **Al Co Ho L**, **P I Ra Te**, **Ag No s Ti C**, etc. If no player can use all their letters, then the one with fewest remaining wins. Incidentally, we remain hopeful that the Cl symbol for chlorine will one day revert back to **M** from muriaticum so that we can write **Ba Na N Ag Ra M S**.

## Banana Stack

This game blends language skill, chance, memory and a smidgen of strategy. Every player takes 20 tiles at random and places them face-down without looking at the letters. They must be mixed thoroughly so no one knows what they have…

Now, the players simultaneously pick up five of their tiles and, keeping them in their hands, try to make the longest word possible. The word must be at least two letters in length. Then, stacking the tiles, they each place their word face-down and declare it, also stating how many tiles they're using – for example, "Four tiles; **FROG!**"

Any tiles that you can't use are tabled face-down alongside your remainder. Each player does this in quick succession to keep up the speed. This also makes it harder to remember which letters you see and where you put them. You must always pick up five tiles; play continues like this until one player uses all of their tiles and wins, or everyone has fewer than five tiles left.

If no one uses all 20 letters then the player with fewest remaining tiles wins. Of course, it's possible that there'll be a draw. In that case, whoever played the most five-letter words wins! If it's still a draw, you can have another go at it and play a tiebreaker!

**Stack of Lies**
Why not add a little duplicity into the game? Banana Stacks lends itself well to an extra dimension in which you may, if you wish, tell one whopping great fib about the letters you play! For example, you might

have only a two-letter word when you stack up a pile of four, claiming the longer word... At any time during the game, opponents may choose to call a player on a suspicious play...

This way, even when a player tells a fib and thinks they're getting away with it, there's still a chance to expose the lie. The only conditions are that, if you're making an accusation, you must do so before you place your tiles down in a round, and you must be specific about which stack you believe contains evidence of the lie! If your accusation proves false, you forfeit your go and must return your letters to your pile.

### ZIP IT®

We're in two minds about mentioning this! On the one hand, it's a game in the same family as BANANAGRAMS and we think it might be seen as a poor show to plug it! On the other hand, ZIP IT® is best described as an ultra-fast, cube-based, two-player version of BANANAGRAMS. Its design means it usually fits inside a large coat pocket, and the game itself can be played on an area as small as an airplane's stowaway table. Many of the tips in *The Little Book of BANANANGRAMS* also apply to ZIP IT®!

# Four Tiebreakers

Every so often whilst playing BANANAGRAMS, two people legitimately call **"BANANAS!"** at the same time! The three games that follow can stand alone, but are of most value when you need a fast tiebreaker.

### Long Bananas

One quick way to resolve a tie is to examine the finished word grids of the players involved. Whichever player created the longest word during the course of the game wins. Obviously, readers of *The Little Book of BANANAGRAMS* might have the natural advantage here anyway… But more so if they set about playing a long word as part of the **IS NEAT** technique… We'll go into this in detail later.

### Chicken Dinner

Quite why some people say, "Winner, winner chicken dinner!" when they win things is debatable: there are several plausible explanations. In any case, **CHICKEN DINNER** serves as the tie-breaking phrase in this approach, which is handy when both potential Top Bananas have the same number of tiles in their longest words. To break the tie, have all the letters put into a face-up **BUNCH**, mix them, and announce that the winner will be whichever player first manages

to find the letters that spell **CHICKEN DINNER**.
Obviously, you can use other words if you'd rather.

## Tropical Mix

Each potential Top Banana thinks of a word with an
agreed number of letters… Somewhere between six and
nine is ideal. You then take the tiles that make up your
word without giving the other player any clue as to what
your word is. Making sure the letters are well scrambled,
put them face-down in front of your opponent. They do
the same… One of you calls "**SPLIT**"; you both turn the
tiles over and race to unscramble each other's words.

## Tournament Tiebreaker

When we stage a tournament, we always have
particular sets of tiles on standby in the event of a tie.
So if you have an extra person in your midst to act as
an adjudicator when two people simultaneously call
"**BANANAS!**", this is the tiebreaker of choice.

The adjudicator takes two identical sets of 21 tiles,
gives one set each to the tied players, face-down, and
mixes them. Now the adjudicator takes two sets of
10 more identical tiles and arranges them face-down.
This is done so that the tiles form a neat column to
one side of each player. It's from these columns that
the two players are going to **PEEL**, and it's imperative
that they're in the same order for both people…

When the adjudicator calls **"SPLIT"**, each player races to turn over and arrange their initial grids. This is the same as a normal game of BANANAGRAMS, but with a pool of pre-determined tiles. When someone shouts **"PEEL"** each player takes the tile that's nearest to them from their own column. In other words, both players have the same tiles when they start and, when they **PEEL**, take identical tiles, in the same order. This can be an incredibly leveling game – all the more so because there's no dumping allowed.

## Tournament Tiebreaker Breakdown

At the time of going to print, these are the letters we tend to put aside as a tiebreaker – but we do change them around a bit. Just be sure that the mix of tiles in each **BUNCH** column offers a balance of consonants and vowels, and has very few – if any – tricky letters.

For each player, remove the following tiles:

**A**3, **B**1, **D**1, **E**4, **G**1, **H**1, **I**3, **L**1, **M**1, **N**2, **O**3, **Q**1, **R**1, **S**2, **T**4, **Y**1, **U**1

From these, we take the letters that spell **MOSTLY GOOD** and use them for the **BUNCH** columns. Remember, these letters are presented in the same order; both players get the **D** first, then an **O** and so on.

# IS NEAT

The N's and S's are comparatively rare in BANANAGRAMS but, as you initially turn over your tiles, it's worth scanning to see if you have all the letters **I, S, N, E, A, T**. You can easily remember them because this tip **IS NEAT**! If you have the full set, you're able to play them alongside any tile except **Q** and **Y** to make a legitimate seven-letter word. Where there's more than one option, we've gone with the more common words! Oh, by the way, these lists are in order of tile commonality rather than alphabetical.

Just **I, S, N, E, A, T** – no other letters:

**TENIAS** – a narrow ribbon or headband

+E   **ETESIAN** – an annual Mediterranean wind

+A   **TAENIAS** – a headband or flat ribbon

+I   **ISATINE** – a compound for preparing dye

+O   **ATONIES** – from **ATONY**: a lack of energy

+T   **INSTATE** – to put a person into a state / condition

+R   **NASTIER** – more nasty

     **RETAINS** – keeps or holds on to

+N   **INANEST** – the most inane

+D   **DETAINS** – hold in custody

     **SAINTED** – of a saint; make a saint

     **STAINED** – marked with color, etc.

+U   **AUNTIES** – more than one Aunt*

+S   **NASTIES** – a group of unpleasant things

+L   **ENTAILS** – involves
        **SALIENT** – most important

+G   **SEATING** – of seats
        **TEASING** – making gentle fun of

+B   **BASINET** – a medieval helmet

+C   **CINEAST** – one who makes films

+F   **NAIFEST** – the superlative form of naïf – naïve

+H   **SHEITAN** – a devilish animal or person

+M   **INMATES** – those occupying prisons, etc.

+P   **PANTIES** – underwear
        **PATINES** – wooden shoes

+J   **JANTIES** – plural of **JANTY**, a Master-at-Arms

+V   **NAIVEST** – the superlative of naïve
        **NATIVES** – indigenous people or things

+W   **TAWNIES** – range of yellowish colors

+K   **INTAKES** – the act of taking something in

+Z   **ZANIEST** – the most zany

+X   **SEXTAIN** – a stanza with six lines

+Q   No help here for the Bananagrammer hoping
        to play a **Q**! That said, if you have a **U** as well
        then you can make **ANTIQUES** or **QUANTISE** –
        meaning old things and wise respectively!

*Perhaps, as a collective noun, it should be a 'fuss' of **AUNTIES**!

The **I, S, N, E, A, T** tiles initially turn up together around one in every four games. Also, if you're struggling to memorize all the words on the list, remember: you ideally want to be getting rid of tricky letters in your first few moves as well. For that reason, you can start getting on top of **IS NEAT** by memorizing only the five words that use difficult tiles: **J, Q** – here with a **U** – **V, X** and **Z**.

# RETINAS

As letter patterns go, this is a heck of a tip – but only if your selection from the **BUNCH** has been uncommonly fortunate! You need to have very few tricky letters in your selection, as well as the letter **R** alongside **IS NEAT** – think **RETINAS**. If that's the case – and it does happen occasionally – then you can play these words:

+E  **TRAINEES** – those being trained
+A  **ANTISERA** – blood serum with antibodies
+I  **RAINIEST** – the most rainy
+O  **NOTARIES** – those empowered to execute legal duties
+T  **TARTINES** – an open sandwich
+R  **STRAINERS** – tools that strain
+N  **ENTRAINS** – board a train

+D **STRAINED** – effortful

+U **URINATES** – wees

+S **RETSINAS** – some Greek wines

+L **ENTRAILS** – guts

+G **ANGRIEST** – the most angry

+B **BANISTER** – part of handrail on stairs

+C **SCANTIER** – more scanty

+H **THERIANS** – group of mammals

+M **RAIMENTS** – clothes

+P **PAINTERS** – people that paint

+W **TINWARES** – plates, etc. made of tin

+K **KERATINS** – proteins found in hair, etc.

The downside of the **RETINAS** pattern is that it lets you use none of the tricky letters, and offers no help with an **F** either. That said, you can use the **Q** in **ANTIQUERS** if you also have a **U**, and all of the others – except **V** – can be played off **RETINAS** as two-letter words if you're desperate.

# Not IS NEAT

An **IS NEAT** move is absolutely the go-to opening technique in BANANAGRAMS on account that it not only uses a really helpful number of tiles but also lets you get rid of at least one tricky letter. But what if you don't have those specific tiles? Here are some other handy combinations to consider. Be careful, though: they don't let you use the tricky letters in the same way that **IS NEAT** does…

# RATIONED

The eight most-common letters in BANANAGRAMS are **A, D, E, I, N, O, R** and **T**. Not particularly memorable presented in alphabetical order like that, but happily they anagram into **RATIONED**. In other words, if you can see at a glance that you have one each of the most common BANANAGRAMS letters, you can play **RATIONED** vertically to get yourself started.[*]

# PARDON

So, the **IS NEAT** letters can combine with all but one letter to make a seven-letter word. Similarly the letters in **PARDON** can combine with all five vowels to make a six-letter word:

+E **APRONED** – having or wearing an apron

+A **PANDORA** – type of mollusc and type of lute

+I **PONIARD** – small, thin dagger

+O **PANDOOR** – soldier in the Croatian army

+U **PANDOUR** – soldier in the Croatian army

[*]If you have **RATIONED** + **Z** then you can play **NOTARIZED**.

# SATIRE

The components of the word **SATIRE** combine with 18 of the 26 letters to make a new six-letter word. Despite taking very few of the tricky letters, the technique still has its moments! As before, the words here are presented in order of commonality:

+E   **SERIATE** – arrange in a series of rows

+A   **ARISTAE** – plural for a beard on grains

+I   **AIRIEST** – the most airy

+T   **TASTIER** – more tasty

+R   **ARTSIER** – more artsy, or arty

+N   **NASTIER** – more nasty

+D   **TIRADES** – angry rants

+S   **SATIRES** – works that mock authority

+L   **RETAILS** – sells in shops

+G   **STAGIER** – more artificial

+B   **BARITES** – samples of a white mineral

+C   **RACIEST** – the most racy; lively

+F   **FAIREST** – the most fair

+H   **HASTIER** – more hasty

+M   **IMARETS** – Turkish hospices for pilgrims

+P   **PARTIES** – social gatherings

+V   **VASTIER** – more vasty, or vast

+W   **WAITERS** – those who serve in restaurants

# U.K. and U.S. Strategies

It's been said that the U.K. and the U.S. are "...two countries separated by a common language." Pithy! But in keeping with the transatlantic confusion, no one's quite sure who actually said it! George Bernard Shaw, James Whistler, Winston Churchill maybe...

In any case, while many U.K. and U.S. words have different meanings or pronunciations, it's really the spellings that concern the Bananagrammer – or should that be Bananagrammar?! Here are some things you might find handy to know – including three strategic reasons to become familiar with U.K. and U.S. word differences...

# Analyze / Analyse

The first is pretty obvious: having a choice between multiple spelling options gives you more opportunities to use the letters that you pick up! No **S**? Play **Z**! Here are some words which – should Lady Luck be kind enough to hand you the tiles – can only end **-YZE** in America... But are spelled **-YSE** in the U.K.

| U.K. | U.S. |
|------|------|
| **ANALYSE** | **ANALYZE** – also **PSYCHOANALYZE** |

| | |
|---|---|
| BREATHALYSE | BREATHALYZE |
| CATALYSE | CATALYZE |
| DIALYSE | DIALYZE |
| ELECTROLYSE | ELECTROLYZE |
| HYDROLYSE | HYDROLYZE |
| PARALYSE | PARALYZE |

# Look into the IZE...

There's often a wailing and gnashing of teeth over words that end with **-ISE** in the U.K. being spelled **-IZE** in the U.S. But in fact **-IZE** is acceptable in many U.K. English words – and at one time was the norm! When you play BANANAGRAMS, there are only a few **-IZE** spellings that neither country accepts. The following words are among the most common; they must always be spelled **-ISE**... Mostly, the other **-ISE** and **-IZE** word are interchangeable:

| U.K. and U.S. | U.K. and U.S. |
|---|---|
| ADVERTISE | COMPROMISE |
| ADVISE | DEMISE |
| APPRISE | DESPISE |
| CHASTISE | DEVISE |
| CIRCUMCISE | DISFRANCHISE |
| COMPRISE | DISGUISE |

| U.K. and U.S. | U.K. and U.S. |
|---|---|
| ENFRANCHISE | PROMISE |
| ENTERPRISE | REVISE |
| EXCISE | SUPERVISE |
| EXERCISE | SURMISE |
| IMPROVISE | SURPRISE |
| INCISE | TELEVISE |
| PREMISE | WISE |

# No S? Play C!

Some folk rightly find it baffling to hear that, where the U.S. just has the word **PRACTICE**, the U.K. spells its verb **PRACTISE** and its noun **PRACTICE**. So **PRACTISE** makes perfect at a dental **PRACTICE**! Some other U.K. nouns end -**ENCE** in the U.K. while U.S. English takes the spelling -**ENSE**... But not expense or intense! Here are the common U.S. -**ENSE** words you may play the other way.

| U.K. | U.S. |
|---|---|
| DEFENCE | DEFENSE |
| LICENCE | LICENSE |
| OFFENCE | OFFENSE |
| PRETENCE | PRETENSE |

# Re: –ER

The second strategy you have at your disposal through knowing the U.K. and U.S. spellings – and agreeing with opponents to allow both – gives you two connection options at the end of a number of words. If you can place letters like F, I, B and E in front of an R on the table more easily than you can play F, I, B, R before an E, then do so! Below are the common words that end -BRE or -TRE in the U.K. but make the switch to -BER and -TER in the U.S.:

| U.K. | U.S. |
|------|------|
| CALIBRE | CALIBER |
| CENTRE | CENTER |
| FIBRE | FIBER |
| LITRE | LITER |
| LOUVRE | LOUVER |
| LUSTRE | LUSTER |
| MANOEUVRE | MANEUVER |
| MEAGRE | MEAGER |
| METRE | METER |
| MITRE | MITER |
| OCHRE | OCHER |
| SABRE | SABER |
| SCEPTRE | SCEPTER |

| U.K. | U.S. |
|---|---|
| **SOMBRE** | **SOMBER** |
| **SPECTRE** | **SPECTER** |
| **THEATRE** | **THEATRE** and **THEATER** |

## Play CENTRE or CENTER

Finally, to illustrate the third U.K. / U.S. strategy, imagine that you're able to play either the word **CENTRE** or the word **CENTER** horizontally in a grid, sharing the **T** with – say – the

vertical word **POTS**. As you probably know, when you play intersecting words in BANANAGRAMS, the letters that end up closest to the cross-section tend to be harder to play off. So, in our example, the proximity of the **O** and **S** in **POTS** is going to render two letters in **CENTRE** / **CENTER** less useful: one is the **N**... The other is going to be either the **R** or the **E** – depending on your choice!

If you play the U.K. spelling, the restriction is on the **R**. In other words, you can more easily play a word that uses the **E**. If you play the U.S. way, the restriction is on the **E** – the **R** is more open... So you need to consider whether you have a better chance of expanding your grid with the **R** on the end, or with the **E**. All other things being equal, it might come down to the fact that more words start with an **R** but more words contain an **E**... And incidentally, assuming you initially take 21 tiles from the **BUNCH**, the distribution of the letters is such that you'll have a **T**, an **E** and an **R** just a little over half of the time... So keep a particular eye out for those **-TRE** / **-TER** words!

# OUR Language

U.K. English words ending **-OUR** tend to finish **-OR** in America. This makes British spelling ideal for babysitting **U**'s that you may need later, and for attaching words to **U**'s that are already in your grid. Here are some common **-OUR** / **-OR** words:

| U.K. | U.S. |
|---|---|
| ARMOUR | ARMOR – also ARMORY |
| BEHAVIOUR | BEHAVIOR |
| CANDOUR | CANDOR |
| CLAMOUR | CLAMOR |
| COLOUR | COLOR |
| DEMEANOUR | DEMEANOR |
| ENDEAVOUR | ENDEAVOR |
| FAVOURITE | FAVORITE |

| U.K. | U.S. |
| --- | --- |
| FLAVOUR | FLAVOR |
| GLAMOUR | GLAMOR |
| HARBOUR | HARBOR |
| HONOUR | HONOR |
| HUMOUR | HUMOR |
| LABOUR | LABOR |
| NEIGHBOUR | NEIGHBOR |
| ODOUR | ODOR |
| RANCOUR | RANCOR |
| RIGOUR | RIGOR |
| RUMOUR | RUMOR |
| SAVIOUR | SAVIOR |
| SAVOUR | SAVOR – also SAVORY |
| SPLENDOUR | SPLENDOR |
| VALOUR | VALOR |
| VAPOUR | VAPOR |
| VIGOUR | VIGOR |

# Give and Take

Ever get really confused between two similar-looking words and end up writing nonsense? Our favorites among such words are **LLAMA** and **LAMA** taken, as we are, with the idea that a shaggy-furred camelid could be mistaken for a monk! Eyeing that extra L makes all the difference, which leads to a useful BANANAGRAMS tactic...

This strategy stems from the British custom of adding an L to words that end with a vowel and one L, when adding a suffix that begins with another vowel. Confused? Understandable! But the example **TRAVEL** makes it clear. In the U.S., the word **TRAVEL** becomes **TRAVELER**, **TRAVELED** or **TRAVELING** when extended, but in the U.K. it's **TRAVELLER**, **TRAVELLED** or **TRAVELLING**... That means the words on this list are ideal for babysitting L's:

| U.K. | U.S. |
|---|---|
| CANCELLING | CANCELING |
| COUNSELLING | COUNSELING |
| EQUALLING | EQUALING |
| FUELLING | FUELING |
| GROVELLING | GROVELING |
| JEWELLERY | JEWELRY |
| LEVELLING | LEVELING |
| LIBELLING | LIBELING |
| MARVELLING | MARVELING |
| MODELLING | MODELING |
| PANELLING | PANELING |

| U.K. | U.S. |
|------|------|
| QUARRELLING | QUARRELING |
| REVELLING | REVELING |
| WOOLLEN | WOOLEN |

In a similar way, the following words are spelled with one **L** in the U.K. – unless being extended – whilst, in the U.S., they always require two. Don't ask us why; we need a long lie down in a cool dark room just writing it up! Or is it down?!

| U.K. | U.S. |
|------|------|
| APPAL | APPALL |
| DISTIL | DISTILL |
| ENROL | ENROLL |
| ENTHRAL | ENTHRALL |
| FULFIL | FULFILL |
| INSTIL | INSTILL |
| SKILFUL | SKILLFUL |
| WILFUL | WILLFUL |

# Double Vowel

Loads of words have double vowels! Just words with double **O**'s could fill a kooky book. **AARDVARK** has the double **A**, **KEEPER** has a double **E**… **BEEKEEPER** has the double **E** twice! The word **SKIING** is the most common playable word that has a double I unhyphenated… Words with **UU** are harder to think of, although **VACUUM** and **CONTINUUM** are common enough. There's also a loose-fitting dress traditionally worn in Hawaii that has the double **U** twice – it's called a **MUUMUU**, pronounced like a cow noise. Twice.

Playing BANANAGRAMS rarely allows you the luxury of a long word, so the chances of needing the U.K. / U.S. spellings relating to the double-vowel combinations **AE** and **OE** are pretty slim… For the sake of completeness though, here are the U.K. words for which the U.S. uses fewer vowels. Again, if they ever come up, they'll babysit the spare letter quite happily!

| U.K. | U.S. |
|---|---|
| **ARCHAEOLOGY** | **ARCHAEOLOGY and ARCHEOLOGY** |
| **LEUKAEMIA** | **LEUKEMIA** |
| **MANOEUVRE** | **MANEUVER** |
| **OESTROGEN** | **ESTROGEN** |
| **PAEDIATRIC** | **PEDIATRIC** |

# OGUE

And finally, there are a few nouns that finish with -**OGUE** in U.K. English that can end with either -**OG** or -OGUE in American use. That makes these words capable of simultaneously babysitting U's, E's and – when pluralized – S's!

| U.K. | U.S. |
|------|------|
| ANALOGUE | ANALOG or ANALOGUE |
| CATALOGUE | CATALOG or CATALOGUE |
| DIALOGUE | DIALOG or DIALOGUE |
| EPILOGUE | EPILOG or EPILOGUE |
| MONOLOGUE | MONOLOG or MONOLOGUE |
| PROLOGUE | PROLOG or PROLOGUE |
| TRAVELOGUE | TRAVELOG or TRAVELOGUE |

With all these different spellings changing the way you play BANANAGRAMS, you might have fun thinking about how one might pronounce the unplayable word 'Ghoti'... The GH could be said like the F sound in rouGH; the O is like the I sound in wOmen and you pronounce the TI the same as the SH sound in naTIon. In other words, 'Ghoti' could be a variant spelling of FISH... Or so some satirical spelling reformer wryly wrote back in the day! The idea of pronouncing the letters 'Ghoti' in this way has been attributed to none other than George Bernard Shaw. Or was it James Whistler? Winston Churchill, maybe...

# Playable Names

When we first wrote *The Little Book of BANANAGRAMS* we didn't entirely appreciate the interest this subject generates! No doubt part of its appeal is down to what life guru Dale Carnegie said about a person's name: that it is, to that person, "...the sweetest, most important sound in any language". There seems to be a more practical reason, too: many of the words on this list are highly memorable – it's much easier to recall an obscure word when it's the name of someone you know!

# What's in a Name?

From Lizzie and Bessy to Libby and Betty, the name Elizabeth has more derivatives than any other moniker in the English language – there are over 50 according to some onomasticians! Interesting though that is, does it help you play BANANAGRAMS? More often than not, yes! That's because quite a few derivatives of Elizabeth are homonyms: they're spelled and pronounced like other words but have different meanings. So you can't play **BET** or **LIB** as a person's name... But you can play them as words meaning 'gamble' and 'castrate' respectively!

You can also play the Elizabeth diminutives **BETH** (a Hebrew letter), **BETTY** (a thief's wrench), **BUFFY** (characterized by buff), **ELSE** (meaning 'other than'), **LILY** (a plant), **LIZA** (a genus of fish), and **LYSSA** (a viral disease, unfortunately, in some animals)! Even leaving out names that one might think of as words first – such as Bob, Chase, Cliff, Dawn, etc. – here are over 100 other names that you can play:

**BARNEY** – an argument

**BASIL** – the herb

**BENEDICT** – a newly-married man

**BILL** – a bird's beak

**BOBBY** – a British policeman

**BONNIE** – pleasing to the eye

**BRAD** – a small nail

**BROOK** – a small stream – and **RILL** means the same thing!

**BUCK** – a dollar

**BUD** – developing flower

**BURL** – knotty outgrowth on a tree

**BUSTER** – informal address for a man

**CAM** – a rotating disc

**CARL** – a man: usually a rude one

**CAROL** – a religious song

**CHANDLER** – a candle maker

**CHARLIE** – a fool

**CHUCK** – to throw away casually

**CORAL** – marine invertebrates

**DAISY** – a flower

**DALE** – a valley

**DAN** – a marker buoy at sea

**DAPHNE** – several types of shrub

**DEAN** – a university administrator

**DIRK** – a long, straight dagger†

**DON** – to put on clothing

**DONNA** – chiefly in Italy, a respectful address for a lady

**EARL** – member of the British nobility

**ERICA** – a genus of plant

**FAITH** – strong belief

**FELICITY** – happiness

**FRANK** – direct

**GENE** – a segment of **DNA**

**GRACE** – elegance

**GRANT** – to give permission

**HANK** – a measure of rope

**HARRY** – to annoy continually

**HAZEL** – a color

**HECTOR** – to bully

**HOLLY** – a shrub

†"Is this a dagger which I see before me?" Well, yes – but it's also known as an obelus. Later, it'll draw your attention to additional remarks in text among which asterisks already frolic. By the way, **OBELUS** is also an anagram of **BLOUSE**, an item of clothing that you don… And **DON** is the name that follows **DIRK**, meaning dagger, in our list!

**IRIS** – part of the eye
**JACK** – a manual laborer
**JADE** – a precious stone
**JASMINE** – a shrub
**JASPER** – precious stone
**JENNY** – female donkey
**JESS** – short strap on a hawk's leg
**JIMMY** – the use of force to open something
**JOCK** – a sporting type
**JOE** – coffee
**JOEY** – baby kangaroo
**JOHN** – toilet
**JOSH** – to joke in good humor
**JOY** – great happiness
**KAT** – leaves of an African shrub
**KAY** – the letter K
**KEN** – knowledge
**KIRK** – a Scottish church
**KITTY** – a communal sum of money
**LANCE** – a long, pointed weapon
**LAUREL** – a wreath of laurel leaves
**MADGE** – a barn owl
**MARIA** – dark regions on the moon
**MARK** – a smudge or blemish
**MARTIN** – any of numerous swallows

**MASON** – a craftsman
**MATT** – not glossy
**MAY** – expression of permission
**MELODY** – a distinct series of musical notes
**MERLE** – a blackbird
**MIKE** – a colloquialism for 'microphone'
**MILES** – units of distance
**MILLER** – a mill worker
**MOIRA** – a person's destiny
**MOLLY** – a type of fish
**NELSON** – a hold in wrestling
**NICK** – small cut or blemish
**NORM** – a statistical term
**OLIVE** – an ovoid fruit, and a tree
**OPAL** – a precious stone
**PATSY** – gullible person
**PATTY** – a mass of chopped food
**PEARL** – a jewel
**PENNY** – a small coin
**PERRY** – a pear cider
**PIP** – a stone or seed
**PIPER** – a pipe player
**POPPY** – a flower
**RAY** – a beam of light
**RICH** – wealthy

**RICK** – a painful muscular twinge
**ROB** – to steal
**ROBIN** – a bird
**ROCKY** – characterized by rocks
**ROD** – a thin implement
**ROGER** – a term for 'message received'
**ROSE** – a flower
**RUBY** – a precious stone
**RUSTY** – eroded by rust
**RUTH** – a feeling of sorrow
**SALLY** – a witty remark
**SANDY** – characterized by sand
**SCARLET** – one T: a red color
**SHEILA** – Australian slang for a girl
**SPENCER** – a thin-knitted vest
**SUE** – to file a suit against
**SYBIL** – a female prophet
**TED** – spread grass out to dry
**TERRY** – a deep-pile cloth
**TIMOTHY** – a long grass used for hay
**TOD** – a unit of weight for wool
**TOM** – a male cat or turkey
**TONY** – high-class
**TREY** – a die / playing card with three spots
**TROY** – a measure for precious metal / gems

**TUCKER** – to tire
**VERITY** – truth
**VICTOR** – a winner
**VIOLET** – a flower
**WADE** – to move through water
**WALLY** – a foolish person
**WARREN** – a burrow
**WILL** – intent
**ZETA** – 6th Greek letter

# Names that are Words that Don't Sound Like Words... or Names!

This list has just a few peculiar words with etymologies relating to people. Later, though, you're going to see a massive list of three-letter words that has been **BOWDLERIZED...** That is to say cleaned up for presentation to a family audience! The word derives from Dr. Thomas Bowdler after he sanitized the works of The Great Bard for publication in a book called *Family Shakespeare*.

**BOYCOTT** – to isolate others; snub them. After Charles Cunningham Boycott – a landlord who, having refused to lower rents for his hapless tenants, was the subject of organized ostracism.

**BOWLER** – Thomas and William Beaulieu, or Bowler, were involved in the production of the stiff, round bowler hat.

**DOILY** – an intricate linen, lace or paper placemat. You don't see a lot of doilies these days but back in the day a man called Doyley kept a linen shop in London, England… It seems to be from here that the word **DOILY** comes.

**GUPPY** – a type of fish, the first specimens of which were noted by one Robert John Lechmore Guppy.

**HERTZ** – unit of frequency. From Heinrich Rudolph Hertz.

**HOOLIGAN** – a ruffian or yob. The word derives either from a notoriously rough family called Houlihan, or from one particularly nasty piece of work named Patrick Hooligan.

**PASCAL** – a unit of pressure equal to one newton per square metre: after Blaise Pascal. A newton, of course, gets its name in the exact same way but from Sir Isaac Newton.

**QUIXOTIC** – overly chivalrous; ridiculously romantic. Derives from the fictional character Don Quixote.

**SPINET** – a harpsichord-like instrument; the invention of Giovanni Spinetti.

**TAWDRY** – meaning cheap and tacky. This is the unfortunate sound-alike legacy of St. Audrey who

wore expensive necklaces in youth. As penance,
it seems she later took to wearing cheap lace –
St. Audrey lace – after developing a tumor on her neck.
Hence, **TAWDRY LACE** and then simply **TAWDRY**.

**YAHOO** – before it was an internet search engine
and a word for a cheer, a yahoo was an disreputable
boor… Named after a tribe of such people, the
Yahoos, in Jonathan Swift's *Gulliver's Travels*.

# Other Proper Nouns

Say "**HOOVER**" in the U.S. and many people think of
J. Edgar, the **FBI**'s first director… Say it in the U.K. and
many people think of sucking up dust! That's because
The Hoover Company once so dominated the U.K.
vacuum-cleaner market that, in some dictionaries, their
brand name became not only a common noun but also
a verb! This list includes other words that one might
imagine are proper nouns and trademarks but that
often appear in dictionaries with a lowercase spelling.

**ASPIRIN** – the drug name is generic

**CATHOLIC** – wide-ranging in taste

**COKE** – a residue left by coal

**GOOGLE** – to use the online search engine Google

**JEEP** – the brand of military vehicle became a generic
term a while ago

**JELLO** – it was a brand name… Now it's a word for the wobbly dessert

**MACE** – the spray is a proper noun… The ceremonial staff is not

**NORTH, SOUTH, EAST, WEST** – the directions aren't always capitalized

**NYLON** – another product that's now a word in itself

**POPSICLE** – U.S. term for a U.K. ice lolly

**PROTESTANT** – one who protests

**SELLOTAPE** – if you have the letters, knock yourself out! It's the U.K. equivalent of Scotch tape

**SPAM** – the meat product was a brand name… But junk email isn't!

**VELCRO** – nowadays, velcro is a verb

**XEROX** – many dictionaries now list this as a photocopy as well as a brand name

## Fabulous Places

As Leslie Bricusse's lyrics from Doctor Dolittle tell us, "There are so many fabulous faraway places to see, Such as Mexico, Sweden, Hawaii, Japan and Capri!" But which of those countries is also a legitimate word that you can play in BANANAGRAMS? The answer is **JAPAN**! How so? Turns out it's a type of varnish… It's the name given to pieces covered with that varnish…

And it's the act of using that varnish! Here's a list relating to places – faraway, fabulous and otherwise – that are also words:

**AFGHAN** – a sheepskin coat

**AFGHANI** – unit of money in Afghanistan

**AMAZON** – a powerful / tall woman

**BABEL** – a confusion of sounds

**BERLIN** – a limousine

**BIKINI** – a bathing suit

**BOLIVIA** – a woollen fabric

**BRAZIL** – a nut; also iron pyrites

**BRIT** – a young herring / sprat

**BURGUNDY** – a color

**CANARY** – a bird

**CAYENNE** – a hot spice

**CELT** – a prehistoric stone axe

**CHAD** – a small scrap of paper

**CHILE** – a pepper, also spelled **CHILI**

**CHINA** – crockery

**COCHIN** – large breed of chicken

**COGNAC** – brandy

**COLOGNE** – perfumed liquid

**CONCORD** – an agreement

**CONGO** – a tea grown in China

**CORDOBA** – monetary unit in Nicaragua

**CURACAO** – an orange flavored liqueur

**CYPRESS** – various evergreen trees

**CYPRIAN** – relating to those who worship Aphrodite

**DAMASK** – a fabric

**DANISH** – a pastry

**DELF / DELFT** – earthenware pottery

**DELPHIC** – ambiguous or obscure

**DERBY** – a type of hat

**DUTCH** – to harden a quill

**ELYSIAN** – blissful or delightful

**ENGLISH** – a spinning motion on a ball

**FLORENCE** – a type of fennel

**FRENCH** – cutting food into strips

**GALILEE** – a porch or vestibule

**GENOA** – a large sail that overlaps the mainsail

**GERMANIC** – pertaining to germanium

**GOA** – it's ¾ of the word **GOAT** – but it's a gazelle!

**GUERNSEY** – a knitted woolen shirt

**GUINEA** – formerly a British coin

**HOLLAND** – a cotton cloth

**JAPAN** – any of several varnishes

**JAVA** – coffee

**JERSEY** – a knitted top

**JORDAN** – a British word for a chamber pot

**KENT** – a long walking staff

**LEVANT** – making a bet intending to abscond if you lose
**LIMA** – a type of bean
**MADRAS** – a cloth
**MANILA** – a form of strong paper
**MECCA** – a place that attracts lots of people
**MOROCCO** – a soft leather
**MUSCAT** – a grape
**PANAMA** – a style of hat
**PHOENIX** – a mythological bird
**PRUSSIC** – pertaining to a type of acid
**ROMAN** – relating to novels written in French
**SAVANNAH** – flat grassland with no trees
**SCOT** – a tax
**SCOTCH** – to stop or put an end to
**SHANGHAI** – to kidnap crew for a ship
**SHETLAND** – a variety of wool
**SWEDE** – the vegetable
**TEXAS** – the upper deck of a steamboat
**TONGA** – a small cart in India
**TURK** – an insect larva
**VALENCIA** – a fabric
**WALES** – ridges left on the skin after being struck
**WARSAW** – a fish: *Epinephelus itajar*

WEORDS

# WEORDS®: Weird Words that Win Word Games (and Wonderful Ways to Work them in!)

It's believed that English playwright William Shakespeare was born on April 23, 1564. Great day! But on the same day 52 years later, he died… A tragedy!* During that time, he developed one of the largest vocabularies of any living man – partly because he made up quite a few words himself. Alas, you can't do that in BANANAGRAMS…

So while the game variations and Sneaky Tips help, it's really vital to have the right vocabulary: one that lets you play tricky tiles, take advantage of transatlantic spellings and use statistically probable letters! The following lists are full of such words and, while we've no desire to reinvent the dictionary, we've given definitions for most of them in case you're challenged. Feel free to take out this book and point to the definitions, too.

Also, you'll see some words pop up in more than one list owing to their construction. **TAV**, for example, appears in the Hebrew alphabet, as a useful three-letter word and, pluralized, as a great way to play a difficult-to-use tile away from the ends of a four-letter word.

*Wouldn't you know it? **GREAT DAY** and **A TRAGEDY** are anagrams of each other!

# Letter Distribution

With just over half of the alphabet distributed throughout **AMBIDEXTROUSLY**, the 14-letter word is one of the longest in which no letter is repeated! Those that play BANANAGRAMS regularly might describe its letter distribution as either 'challenging' or 'infuriating'… How any one person feels about it largely depends on whether they routinely win or lose! The distribution is as follows:

| | | | | | | |
|---|---|---|---|---|---|---|
| A13 | B3 | C3 | D6 | E18 | F3 | G4 |
| H3 | I12 | J2 | K2 | L5 | M3 | N8 |
| O11 | P3 | Q2 | R9 | S6 | T9 | U6 |
| V3 | W3 | X2 | Y3 | Z2 | | |

# Statistically Likely

Now, you might not have given it much thought, but you can see the game contains just six **S** tiles in spite of the fact that more English words start with **S** than any other letter! And as you know, you can also put an **S** on the end of many nouns and verbs… So the calculated rarity of the **S** in BANANAGRAMS adds to the frenetic nature of the game.

Meanwhile, there's a small group of words that you can make using a selection from the most common letters in BANANAGRAMS – **A**, **E**, **I**, **O**, **R** and **T**. So words on these lists are quite likely to be immediately playable when you first turn over your tiles. And keep in mind that, while many of them are four-letter words – not long enough to get you off the starting blocks in style – some, like **RIOT**, might easily extend to a more helpful length by adding **-S**, **-ER**, **-ED**, **-ING** or **-OUS**. Also, you'll see asterisks next to a few of the words. They indicate that the word contains a difficult-to-play tile away from the start or end of it – helpful when playing 'Steps'. Henceforth, the obelus (†) directs your attention to footnotes. Finally, you'll see that even the simplest words have a broad definition. That's to be complete rather than because we think everything needs éclaircissement.†

**AIRT** – a direction

**IOTA** – a tiny amount

**RATE** – speed

**RIOT** – unruly mob of people

**RITE** – a solemn ceremony

**ROTA** – schedule

**ROTE** – the roaring noise of the sea

**ROTI** – a type of bread

**TARE** – weight of equipment in vehicle

**TARO** – type of edible plant

†Clarification!

**TEAR** – rip

**TIER** – layer

**TIRE** – rubber ring on a wheel

**TIRO** – a learner

**TOEA** – currency in Papua New Guinea

**TORA** – an antelope

**TORI** – gateway by a Japanese shrine

More interesting are the five-letter words you can make from the most common letters: **IRATE, OATER, ORATE, RATIO, RETIA, TERAI**. The words **OATER**, **RETIA** and **TERAI** mean a western-style film, the plural of **RETE** and a wide-brimmed hat respectively!

# Statistically Likely Plus

Here's a variety of mostly five-or-more-letter words that you can create from among the most common tiles plus one other! There's a good chance you can make a five, six, or seven-letter word in a very short amount of time, playing it as a first or second word. Those words that have an asterisk by them use a more difficult-to-play-letter toward the middle of the word... Useful for playing 'Steps'.

**AEIORT +E**
**AERIE** – the nest of a bird of prey
**ARÊTE** – ascending ridge of mountain

**AEIORT + A**
**AORTA** – a main circulatory artery
**AORTAE** – the plural of **AORTA**
**REATA** – rope for tethering and catching animals
**TIARA** – an ornamental headband

**AEIORT +I**
**TORII** – gateway by a Japanese shrine

**AEIORT +O**
**ROOT** – part of plant that absorbs nourishment

**AEIORT +R**
**AIRER** – frame on which clothes are aired
**ARTIER** – more **ARTY!**
**RATER** – that which rates a thing
**RETRO** – belonging to a time past
**TRIER** – one who examines a cause

**AEIORT +T**
**ATTIRE** – clothing
**OTTER** – water-dwelling mammal

**ROTATE** – spin
**TAROT** – cards used to tell fortunes
**TREAT** – attend to
**TRITE** – worn out by overuse, as with a phrase

**AEIORT +N**
**ANTRE** – a cavern or cave
**ATONE** – to make amends
**INERT** – having no motion
**IRONE** – a fragrant oil
**ORANT / ORANTE** – an image or representation of
  a person worshipping with their arms outstretched
**ORNATE** – elaborately decorated
**RATION** – limited amount of supplies
**RETAIN** – hold on to
**TENIA / TEANIA** – a headband, or flat ribbon
**TENOR** – a male singing voice
**TONIER** – having a more fashionable tone
**TRAIN** – public transport vehicle

**AEIORT +D**
**ADROIT** – clever or resourceful
**AIRED** – having air
**AIRTED** – set moving in a particular direction
**DROIT** – a legal right

**EDITOR** – one who edits

**OARED** – having oars

**ORATED** – prayed; pleaded

**RADIO** – broadcasting system

**RIOTED** – past tense of riot; disturbance by unruly mob

**ROADIE** – person who sets up then puts away a music band's equipment

**TARDO** – of music: to be played slowly

**TIRADE** – a vehement speech

**TIRED** – physical or mental fatigue

**TRIED** – attempted

**TREAD** – top board on a stair

**TRIAD** – a group of three

**AEIORT +U**

**AUREI** – Roman gold coins

**OURIE** – cheerless as a result of illness

**OUTER** – located externally

**ROUTE** – way from one place to another

**URATE** – salt from uric acid

**UTERI** – plural of uterus

**AEIORT +S**

**ARIOSE** – song-like; melodic

**ARISE** – to get up

**AROSE** – got up!

**IOTAS** – plural of **IOTA** the Greek letter I

**OSIER** – any of several willow trees, or their twigs

**RAISE** – lift or increase

**RITES** – solemn ceremonies

**ROAST** – cook slowly

**ROTAS** – schedules

**SATIRE** – humor at the expense of the establishment

**SITAR** – a guitar-like, Indian instrument

**SORTIE** – a swift movement by the military

**STAIR** – a step

**STOAE** – covered walkways in ancient Greece

**STORE** – shop; also to keep for later use

**TARSI** – err on the side of caution: the safest
   definition is the plural of **TARSUS**; an ankle bone

**TIERS** – layers

**TIRES** – rubber rings on wheels

**TRIES** – attempts

**TOISE** – a French measurement of length

**AEIORT +L**

**ALERT** – notify

**ALTER** – adjust

**LATER** – a point in time after now

**LITER** – a measurement; often for liquid

**LITRE** – a measurement; often for liquid

**LOITER** – wait about idly

**OILER** – a person or device that oils

**RETAIL** – sell in stores

**TAILOR** – one who makes clothes

**TELOI** – plural of Telos: an end goal

**TILER** – one who tiles

**TRAIL** – lag behind or linger

**TRIAL** – the act of testing something or someone

**AEIORT +G**

**ARGOT** – the language of a profession

**ERGOT** – a diseased rye seed

**GAITER** – protective leggings

**GAROTE** – a method of execution

**GETA** – a wooden shoe

**GOAT** – not a particularly useful word, but check out the pupils in a goat's eyes. Amazing!

**GOITER / GOITRE** – a swelling of the neck

**GRATE** – to shred

**GREAT** – super; also enormous

**GROAT** – an old English coin

**TIGER** – a wild cat

**TOGAE** – the plural of Toga

**TRIAGE** – determining medical priorities
**TRIGO** – wheat

**AEIORT +B**
**ABORT** – end prematurely
**BARITE** – a mineral
**BIOTA** – animals and plants, collectively
**BITER** – one who bites
**BOATER** – one who uses a boat
**BOITE** – a small club or restaurant
**ORBIT** – travel around
**TRIBE** – a group of people
**TABOR** – a drum

**AEIORT +C**
**ACTOR** – one who plays a role
**CARET** – the ∧ mark that shows text is missing
**CATER** – prepare / supply food at an event
**COATI** – a raccoon-like mammal
**CRATE** – packing case
**EROTIC** – relating to physical love
**EROTICA** – material relating to physical love
**ICER** – one who ices such as on a cake
**REACT** – respond to
**RECTO** – a page on the right in a book!
**RICE** – staple food

**TORIC** – relating to a ring-shaped surface
**TRACE** – go over or track down
**TRICE** – a short moment

**AEIORT +F**
**AFIRE** – on fire
**AFORE** – a time before; earlier
**AFRIT** – a powerful demon
**AFTER** – following
**FETOR** – the smell of decay
**FORTE** – specialty
**REFIT** – renew for use again

**AEIORT +H**
**AIRTH** – a direction
**EARTH** – the planet on which most of us live
**HEART** – major organ that pumps blood round the body
**HERIOT** – after death, a payment made to a lord by
  tenants… Usually in livestock
**HIERA** – plural of **HIERON**, a temple
**OTHER** – not this
**THEIR** – belonging to others
**THORIA** – the oxide of thorium

**AEIORT +M**
**AMORT** – lifeless or inanimate

**IMARET** – Turkish travelers' hospice

**MATER** – word for mother

**METRO** – underground train system in various countries

**MERIT** – a valuable quality

**MITER / MITRE** – a right-angled joint

**MOIRE** – a fabric

**MORAE** – plural of **MORA**, a unit of time based on syllables

**OMERTA** – a refusal to talk openly about something. We'll say no more…

**RAMIE** – a herbaceous plant

**REMIT** – an area of responsibility

**TAMER** – one who tames animals

**TIMER** – device that measures time

**TOMIA** – plural of **TOMIUM**: the cutting edge on a bird's beak

**AEIORT +P**

**APORT** – on a ship; towards the portside

**OPERA** – drama set to music

**OPIATE** – drug that sedates, or dulls the senses

**PATER** – father

**PATIO** – paved area in a garden, usually attached to a house

**PIRATE** – one who robs at sea

**PRATE** – to chatter idly

**PROTEI** – plural of proteus, bacteria in your digestive system

**REPOT** – to put a plant into a different pot

**TAPER** – narrow gradually

**TAPIR** – a mammal that looks like a cross between a long-nosed pig and a horse

**TRIPE** – an animal's stomach lining used for cooking

**AEIORT +J**

**JIAO** – a Chinese coin / currency

**JOTA** – a folk dance in Spain

**AEIORT +V**

**AVERT*** – to turn away

**OVATE*** – egg-shaped

**OVERT*** – done openly

**RAVE*** – support enthusiastically

**RIVET*** – a secure fastening; also the liver of a fish!

**TROVE*** – a valuable find

**VIATOR** – a traveler

**VIREO** – a small songbird

**VOTER** – one who casts a voter or ballot

*Remember, the words with an asterisk in these lists use the more difficult letters towards the middle.

**AEIORT +W**
**TAWIE** – easy to manage
**TOWER** – a tall, thin building
**TOWIE** – in Australia, a tow truck!
**WAITER** – one who serves in restaurants
**WART** – fleshy protuberance on the body
**WATER** – $H_2O$
**WRITE** – express with words on paper
**WROTE** – past tense of write

**AEIORT +Y**
**TEARY** – tearful
**TOYER** – one who plays with toys

**AEIORT +K**
**KRAIT** – a type of poisonous snake
**OKRA** – a tall plant
**TAROK** – another word for tarot
**TRIKE** – to hang or flow downward
**TROIKA** – three associated powerful people or groups
**TROKE** – to fail and be left wanting, as when losing
  BANANAGRAMS

The Q-without-a-U is of almost no use in the context of this list! You're best advised to play a Q-without-a-U word and focus on the other common letters separately. If you have common letters and a **U** though, there are plenty of five-letter words that begin with **QU**. As you may know from 'So It Begins', the **QU** at the start of a word isn't ideal. Here are some words that bury it nearer the middle.

**AEIORT +QU**

**EQUATOR\*** – imaginary line around a planet 'marking out' the hemispheres

**ROQUE\*** – a variation of croquet

**ROQUET\*** – a type of lizard and a stroke in croquet

**TORQUE\*** – a twisting force

**AEIORT +Z**

**AZOTE\*** – a name for nitrogen

**TZAR\*** – formerly, the emperor of Russia

**ZETA** – sixth letter in the Greek alphabet

**ZOEA** – crustaceans in larval form

**ZORI** – another sandal made of wood[†]

**AEIORT +X**

**EXIT\*** – way out

**EXTRA\*** – more than required

**IXORA\*** – a shrub

**OXTER\*** – the arm hole in a coat!

**TAXI\*** – form of transport that vanishes when it rains

[†]We're not sure what the difference is between **ZORI**, **PATINES** and **GETA** but **ZORI** seems to be the hardest wood.

Finally, a special mention to the word **TAXI** from the **X** list… Not only because it's one of the most recognizable words anywhere in the world, but also because it's suffered from swingeing reductions over the years! You see, **TAXI** and **CAB** both came from **TAXICAB**… Before which **TAXICAB** came from the French, '**TAXIMETER CABRIOLET**'.

# Alphabets

One of the very first things we're ever taught is the alphabet… But why is it called that? Well, it derives from the first two Greek letters: **ALPHA, BETA**! Along with the rest of the Greek letter names, these words come in pretty handy, as do some of the official spellings for the Roman and Hebrew letters. Notice how a number of the shorter words have unusual letter combinations.

**Greek**

| | | | |
|---|---|---|---|
| ALPHA | ETA | NU | TAU |
| BETA | THETA | XI | UPSILON |
| GAMMA | IOTA | OMICRON | PHI |
| DELTA | KAPPA | PI | CHI |
| EPSILON | LAMBDA | RHO | PSI |
| ZETA | MU | SIGMA | OMEGA |

## Roman

It's always struck us as odd that the letters of the Roman alphabet, when spelled out, omit the major vowels! **A** and **I** are words in themselves, though, and the manner in which one might spell **O** and **U** are also words: **OH** and **YOU**! That just leaves **E** unaccounted for in the alphabet – along with the very unhelpful **W**, which could arguably be spelled double-you!

| | | | |
|---|---|---|---|
| BEE | AITCH | EN | TEE |
| CEE | JAY | PEE | VEE |
| DEE | KAY | CUE | EX |
| EF | EL | AR | WYE |
| GEE | EM | ES / ESS | ZED / ZEE |

## Hebrew

| | | |
|---|---|---|
| ALEF / ALEPH | TET / TETH | PE / PEH |
| BET / BETH | YOD | TSADI / SADHE / SADE |
| GIMEL | KAF / KAPH | |
| DALET / DALETH | LAMED / LAMEDH | KOPH / QOPH |
| HE / HEH | MEM | RESH |
| VAV | NUN | SHIN / SIN |
| ZAYIN | SAMEKH | TAV |
| HET / CHETH | AYIN | |

# Animal. Vegetable. Mineral.

The word **LAMINA** applies to a sensitive tissue in a horse's hoof, a thin layer in minerals and the flat part of a leaf... In other words, it relates to animals, minerals and vegetables! It's also, happily, an anagram of **ANIMAL**. And it's the animal kingdom we first visit for some handy words, with the other categories following...

## Animal

**CAVY** – a Patagonian **MARA**

**DUGONG** – a walrus-like mammal

**FOSSA** – a long-tailed wildcat

**GERENUK** – a long necked, tiny-headed antelope

**KUDU** – some African antelopes share this name

**MARA** – a couple of burrowing rodents have the name!

**OKAPI** – a large mammal with a brown body but black and white striped legs

**OLM** – a cave-dwelling salamander

**PACU** – a type of fish

**SQUAB** – a boon to all word-game players: it's a young pigeon!

**QUAGGA** – an extinct horse / zebra hybrid

**QUOLL** – a marsupial in Australia, New Guinea and Tasmania

**SAIGA** – a Russian antelope
**ZEBU** – a hump-backed ox

**Plant**
**ALFALFA** – leguminous plant in Asia
**AXIL** – angle between a branch and the trunk it's on
**KUDZU** – an East Asian climbing plant
**GINKGO** – a tree in China and Japan
**XYLEM** – part of a tree that carries nutrients from the
   roots to the leaves
**WHORL** – leaves / branches that wrap round stems
**SEPAL** – the part of a bloom that supports petals
**TEPAL** – an outer part of a flower – and an anagram
   of petal

Finally, a special mention to the word **BLOSSOM**, which
is a fantastic example of what's known as a Kangaroo
Word. What the dickens does that mean? Well, in the
same way that kangaroos carry their young in a pouch,
a Kangaroo Word carries within it a smaller word that
relates to itself... If you're still none the wiser, take the
two **S**'s out of **BLOSSOM** and see what you get!

**Mineral**
**CARAT** – U.K. spelling of **KARAT**: measure of gold
**CULET** – horizontal face of diamonds when cut as
   'brilliant'

**DRUSE** – small crystals on an inner surface of rock

**LOESS** – yellowy / brown loamy deposit

**MICA** – rock-forming minerals

**QUARTZ** – with **QUA** being a word that means 'in the capacity of…', **QAT** being a shrub, and **QUART** being a measurement, it's easy to see why the mineral **QUARTZ** is a handy word to remember!

**SCHIST** – metamorphic rocks that can be split in layers

**TALC** – soft mineral used to make talcum powder

# Abbreviations

It would be apt if we kept this list short, wouldn't it? Easily done since most abbreviations are disallowed in word games. There are, however, some abbreviations that have become so common as to work their way into the dictionary anyway. Here are some that have handy letter combos:

**AB** – abdominal muscle

**AD; ADVERT** – advertisement

**AG** – agriculture

**AWOL** – Absent Without Leave

**ED** – education

**LASER** – Light Amplification by the Stimulated Emission of Radiation

**OFFIE** – an Off License; a shop that sells alcohol in the U.K.

**POMO** – Post Modern

**QUANGO** – Quasi Autonomous Non Governmental Organization; also **QANGO**

**RADAR** – Radio Detection And Ranging

**SCUBA** – Self Contained Underwater Breathing Apparatus

**TASER** – Tom Swift's Electric Rifle

**WOOPIE** also **WOOPY** – Well Off Older Person

**ZA** – pizza

Finally, we call attention to the ghastly word **YUPPIE**... This 80s-born travesty is remembered as meaning Young Upwardly Mobile Professional, even though that clearly spells **YUMP**. However, a **YUMP** is the action of a speeding rally car momentarily leaving the ground. **YUMPIE** is the abbreviation derived from Young Upwardly Mobile Professional, while **YUPPIE** actually stood for Young Urban Professional, even though there were three unnecessary letters in the acronym. But is **YUP** a real word? Why, yes it is! It means 'yes', as in "Have you had enough of the abbreviations?" "Yup..."

# Two-Letter Words

Would you describe your vocabulary as grandiloquent? Let's hope not – it means 'pompous and inflated'! And while a vocabulary of fancy words sometimes helps in BANANAGRAMS, more often than not it's short words that save the day. Remember to play two-letter words off the middle of longer words rather than near the beginning or end! The following two-letter words fit quickly into a BANANAGRAMS grid and many are quite easy to memorize…

From here on, by the way, eagle-eyed language lovers might see some words populating more than one list. For example, **XU** is a particularly useful two-letter word that we mention in both the **X** / vowel list and the Alphabet section… Obviously, though, it also appears among all the two-letter words, despite it not particularly standing out there. To kick us off, here are some words that babysit vowels…

# Six Wonderful Words that Babysit Vowels

Every so often, you need to get rid of a few vowels quickly. You don't have time to rebuild your whole grid; you need to put down a tile fast – then reassess!

Here are six excellent two-letter words that let one vowel 'babysit' another until they're needed elsewhere.

**AA** – in Hawaii, this is volcano lava that has set with a rough, jagged surface

**AE** – in Scotland, this is a word meaning 'one'

**AI** – a three-toed sloth. Sounds like we made it up, but it's true!

**OE** – in Scotland, a grandchild. Its variant spellings are also useful: **OY** and **OYE**

**OI** – a cry to get attention

**OU** – in Hawaii, a bird

# A Lot of Two-Letter Words

According to research by some very clever folk at Oxford University, a whopping 25% of the content written and spoken in English consists of just ten words... Put another way, one in every four words people use is: the, be, to, of, and, a, in, that, have and I. Imagine that! Those ten words are doing a quarter of all the work...

In any case, it all goes to show how hard the little words work. That's also true in BANANAGRAMS of course, and while there are some very common two-letter words that we really don't think you'd need explaining, we've included them for the sake of completeness.

Then there are the weirder words. Many of those absolutely do need defining on account that they look like someone let a monkey poke at a keyboard. It's a pretty long list – 120 words in total. Sounds like a lot! When you break it down, though, you'll find it's made up as follows:

31 everyday words – you almost certainly already know them

20 exclamations – if it's a sound from your mouth, someone has probably spelled it

10 alphabet words – you immediately understand why they're words

9 musical notes

50 truly weird words that might need more effort to remember!

**AA** – in Hawaii, hardened lava

**AB** – abdominal muscle

**AD** – advertisement

**AE** – Scottish word: one

**AG** – exclamation of disgust

**AH** – expression of surprise

**AI** – a three-toed sloth

**AL** – a shrub

**AM** – exist: present tense of be

**AN** – indefinite article before vowel sounds

**AR** – the letter R

**AS** – whilst

**AT** – indicator of location

**AW** – affectionate sound

**AX** – an axe

**AY** – a yes vote

**BA** – Egyptian spirit

**BE** – exist

**BI** – attracted to both sexes

**BO** – address for a man

**BY** – beside

**DA** – Burmese knife

**DE** – of or from

**DI** – musical tone

**DO** – take action

**EA** – U.K. dialect: a river

**ED** – education

**EE** – Scottish: an eye

**EF** – the letter F

**EH** – questioning sound

**EL** – the letter L; elevated railway

**EM** – the letter M

**EN** – the letter N

**ER** – exclamation of hesitation
**ES** – the letter S
**EX** – former
**FA** – musical note
**FY** – digest
**GI** – material arts suit
**GO** – depart
**GU** – a musical instrument
**HA** – sound of laughing
**HE** – male of species
**HI** – hello
**HM** – pensive sound
**HO** – a deep laugh
**ID** – unconscious instincts
**IF** – in the event
**IN** – inside
**IO** – exclamation of triumph
**IS** – exists, present tense
**IT** – object or animal
**JA** – in South Africa, 'yes'
**JO** – sweetheart
**KA** – Egyptian spirit
**KI** – energy in martial arts
**KO** – a digging stick

**KY** – Scottish plural of cow
**LA** – musical note
**LI** – Chinese unit of weight
**LO** – look
**MA** – mother
**ME** – reference to self
**MI** – musical note
**MM** – pensive sound
**MO** – moment
**MU** – 12th Greek letter
**MY** – belonging to self
**NA** – no
**NE** – formerly known as
**NO** – expression of the negative
**NU** – 13th Greek letter
**OB** – a magician
**OD** – a mystical force
**OE** – a small island
**OF** – belonging to
**OH** – sound of surprise
**OI** – call to get attention
**OM** – meditative sound
**ON** – attached or atop
**OO** – in Hawaii, a bird

**OP** – military operation
**OR** – alternatively
**OS** – connective tissue
**OU** – a man
**OW** – exclamation of pain
**OX** – a bull
**OY** – call to get attention
**PA** – father
**PE** – 17th Hebrew letter
**PI** – 16th Hebrew letter
**PO** – a bedpan
**QI** – a Chinese life force
**RE** – musical note
**SH** – sound to hush others
**SI** – musical note
**SO** – therefore
**ST** – the same as **SH!**
**TA** – thanks
**TE** – musical note
**TI** – musical note
**TO** – expressing movement
**UG** – fear or dread
**UH** – sound of hesitation
**UM** – sound of hesitation

**UN** – one; as in "a big un"

**UP** – overhead

**UR** – exclamation of uncertainty

**US** – you and I

**UT** – musical note

**WE** – you and I

**WO** – archaic spelling of woe

**XI** – 14th Greek letter

**XU** – currency in Vietnam

**YA** – you

**YE** – Old English: those being addressed

**YO** – a salutation

**YU** – Chinese wine vessel

**ZA** – slang term for pizza

**ZO** – a Tibetan yak / cow hybrid

Musketeers. Little Pigs. Blind Mice. As the band Schoolhouse Rock tells us, three is a magic number! And they're everywhere: in The Bit at the Back of the Book, you'll discover an enormous list that one can easily make out of the two-letter words you just saw. Here, though, are some three-letter words you might find most valuable straight away: those that let you get rid of the letters J, Q, V, X or Z…

# Three-Letter Words

Whilst only two two-letter words let you shift the **J** quickly – **JA** and **JO**, explained earlier – there are a few more with three, including the common words **JAB**, **JAM**, **JAR**, **JAW**, **JET**, **JOB**, **JOG**, **JOT**, **JOY**, **JUG**. There is only one three-letter word with a **J** in the middle: **AJI**. It's a chili pepper! And here are two more lists: 'Starts with a **J**' and 'Ends with a **J**'…

# J-Words

**Starts with a J**

**JAG** – a rough edge

**JAK** – jackfruit: a fruit

**JAY** – type of bird

**JEE** – an amazed interjection

**JEU** – French word for a game

**JIB** – a **GIB**: bonding pin or screw

**JIG** – dance

**JIN** – also **JINN**: a demon

**JOE** – coffee

**JOW** – the ringing of a bell

**JUN** – North Korean monetary unit

**JUS** – a thin gravy
**JUT** – stand out or proud

**Ends with a J**
**RAJ** – in India, the time of British rule
**TAJ** – a high, conical cap

# Q-Words

**Starts with a Q**
**QAT** – a shrub
**QIN** – in China, a stringed instrument
**QIS** – plural of **QI**; a life energy
**QUA** – by virtue of being

**Ends with a Q**
Only a couple of three-letter words end with a **Q**.
The first is an Arab market called a **SUQ**, pronounced
to rhyme with **NUKE**. The other is **COQ**, which is a
feather worn in a lady's hat.

# V-Words

You can't spell **VERSATILE** without **V** and **TILE**!
But the poor old **V** is often reviled as one of the
hardest letters to use quickly, since it doesn't appear in

any legitimate two-letter words. But there are plenty of three-letter words! Again, we've included broad definitions for simple words even if we don't think they necessarily need epexegesis.[†]

### Starts with a V

**VAC** – vacuum cleaner

**VAE** – woe

**VAN** – vehicle for moving goods

**VAR** – a unit of power

**VAS** – a vessel or duct

**VAT** – a large container

**VAU**, **VAV** and **VAW** – the 6th Hebrew letter

**VEE** – the letter V

**VEG** – a vegetable

**VET** – a veterinarian

**VEX** – to irritate or annoy

**VIA** – by way of

**VID** – informally 'video'

**VIE** – to compete

**VIG** – vigorish

**VIM** – energy

**VIN** – wine

[†]This is another posh word for explanation… But its alternating vowel / consonant construction makes it an absolute beauty!

**VIS** – strength / force
**VOE** – in Orkney, Scotland, a creek
**VOL** – two wings joined at the base
**VOM** – to vomit; be sick
**VOW** – a solemn promise
**VOX** – a voice
**VUG** – a rock cavity

## V in middle
**AVA**[*] – Scottish for 'at all'
**AVE**[*] – welcome / farewell
**AVO**[*] – currency in Macao
**EVE**[*] – the night before a big day
**IVY**[*] – a climbing plant
**OVA**[*] – the plural of ovum

## Ends with a V
**DEV / DIV** – an evil Persian spirit
**GUV** – informal name for governor
**HAV** – haversine; a trigonometrical function in maths
**LEV** – Bulgarian monetary unit
**LUV** – love
**REV** – revolution per minute
**TAV / VAV** – Hebrew letters

[*]Remember, the words with an asterisk in these lists use the more difficult letters towards the middle.

# X-Words

X is arguably the most mysterious letter! It promises value when it marks the spot, and it represents the unknown not only in Files and Factors but also in algebra and science! If you play BANANAGRAMS a lot, though, you'll really appreciate this one well-kept secret about **X**... When you put it next to any major vowel, it makes a two-letter word! But **AX**, **EX**, **XI**, **OX** and **XU** are not the only handy X-words! As well as the obvious three-letter X-words – **BOX**, **FAX**, **FIX**, **FOX**, **MAX**, **MIX**, **POX**, **SIX**, **SEX**, **TAX**, **WAX** – there are some that are more unusual...

**Starts with an X**
**XIS** – plural of **XI**: 14th Greek letter

**X in the middle**
**AXE**[*]

**Ends with an X**
**COX** – a person shouting to a team of rowers
**DUX** – a leader or chief
**GOX** – gaseous oxygen
**HEX** – to bewitch
**KEX** – the stem of many herbaceous plants
**LAX** – not strict
**LEX** – a system of laws

**LOX** – a smoked salmon

**LUX** – a unit of illumination

**NIX** – to reject or cancel

**PAX** – in Christianity, a sign of peace

**PIX** – photographs

**PYX** – a container in which a church keeps consecrated bread

**RAX** – straining and stretching

**REX** – in the U.K., part of a king's official title

**SAX** – saxophone

**SOX** – socks

**TEX** – unit used to measure yarn

**TUX** – informal word for tuxedo

**VEX** – to irritate or annoy

**VOX** – a voice

**ZAX** – a tool for trimming slates

# Z-Words

If **VEX**, **VOX** and **ZAX** didn't end our X list, they'd still appear on the **V** or **Z** lists respectively! Common three-letter Z-words include **ZAP**, **ZED**, **ZEE**, **ZIP**, **ZIT**, **ZOO** and – while they're usually seen together – you can, of course, play **ZIG** and **ZAG** as individual words. The weirder **Z WEORDS** are:

## Starts with a Z

**ZAS** – plural of **ZA**, an abbreviation of pizza

**ZEA** – the grain **SPELT**

**ZEK** – in Russia, a prison camp inmate

**ZOA** – a biology term; relates to defining 'animals'

**ZUZ** – ancient Hebrew coin

## Z in the middle

**AZO*** – relates to specific ions / molecules

Earlier talk of the Tibetan yak / cow hybrid, the **ZO**, may lead you to think it's so specific a thing that there could only possibly be one word for it. Not so! The exact same animal is also spelled **ZHO**, **ZOBO**, **ZOBU**, **DZO*†** and **DZHO**.*† Typical... You wait ages for one name of a Tibetan cattle crossbreed, then six come along all at once!

## Ends with a Z

**ADZ** – an axe-like tool

**BIZ** – business

**COZ** – cousin

**CUZ** – a term meaning 'family member'

**FEZ** – a felt cap

**POZ** – informally; certain

**WIZ** – a wizard

†Remember, the words with an asterisk in these lists use the more difficult letters towards the middle.

To round off our festival of three-letter words, we mention a curious challenge which tasks wordsmiths to construct a grammatically sound sentence with as many consecutive uses of the word **HAD** as possible... A lot of people get to 11. Our own version has 14! It employs the contextual device of two friends, Chloe and Gary, each being asked to write a sentence using the verb 'had'. Here goes... Gary, where Chloe had had 'had', had had 'had had' – had 'had had' had 'had had', 'had', or any other number of 'hads' in front of it, it would've made no sense!

# Q without U

Fewer than one in every 500 letters in written English is a **Q**. Indeed, by some scales only **Z** is less common, although some would argue **Z**, **J** and **Q** are all slugging it out for the dubious distinction of being the least-used letter... But of course, a **Q**'s scarcity isn't the only problem: the fact that it so often needs a **U** to get rid of it means there's almost always a huff, groan, or colorful metaphor when it's peeled. Here's a list of **Q** words that don't use a **U**:

**CINQ**; alternative spelling of **CINQUE** – five on dice or cards

**FAQIR** – an Islamic monk

**FIQH** – the study of Islamic religious law

**INQILAB** – in India; revolution

**NIQAB** – a veil for the lower face

**QABALA** – a form of Judaism

**QADI** – a Muslim judge

**QAID** – a Muslim tribal chief

**QANAT** – underground tunnel

**QASIDA** – an Arabic verse form

**QAWWAL** – a singer of Islamic religious songs:
  **QAWWALI**

**QI** – an energy

**QIBLA** – toward Mecca

**QIBLI** – Mediterranean wind

**QIGONG** – a Chinese breathing exercise

**QINTAR / QINDAR** – win word games with two
  spellings of the Albanian currency

**QOPH** – Hebrew letter

**QORMA** – alternative spelling of **KORMA** – a curry

**QWERTY** – the standard English keyboard layout

**SHEQALIM** – the plural of sheqel

**SHEQEL** – currency of Israel

**TALAQ** – a form of Islamic divorce

**TZADDIQ** – Jewish spiritual leader

**WAQF** – endowing property to a religious institution

**YAQONA** – Fijian for **KAVA**; a Polynesian shrub

### Hard QIS

Was it comedian Craig Shoemaker who said the words Feng Shui translate into "Putting your husband's rubbish in the garage"? Either way, it's Feng Shui's rise in popularity that we have to thank for many English dictionaries including the words **CHI** and **QI**, defining them as a life force. You're allowed the plurals as well, by the way, but here's the rub – after you play **QI** you tend to be stuck with it... Other than **QIS**, **QI** is a hard word to expand!

What's needed here is a little opposite thinking: if – having put **QI** in your grid – you later pick up a **U**, don't hesitate to find a spare **D**, **N**, **P**, or **T** in your grid, and extend **QI** to **QUID**, **QUIN**, **QUIP** or **QUIT**. The reason being that, if you need to, you can later swap out the last letter for a **Z**. In other words, instead of using an **I** just to get rid of a **Q**, you can plan to lose a **Z** there as well.

## But that's Not All!

As the sales blurb often says, there's more! It's worth noting that **QUIZ** instantly turns into another word when it takes an **S** on the front: **SQUIZ**... In New Zealand, it means to glance, or look at something quickly. The reason this is so valuable is simply that it tees you up to get rid of the second **Z**. If you pick it up, you only need free up one **E** to place **QUIZZES**.

# May the Fours be with You

The only number that, when spelled as a word, has the same amount of letters as the word indicates is **FOUR**. And while this book spends quite a bit of time looking at the importance of two- and three-letter words, we shouldn't overlook the value of four-letter words earlier in the game. When you create your initial grid, building Steps of four or more tiles gives you more space: it helps you avoid Gridlock. Each of these lists features words that use tricky tiles but keep them away from the ends so that your Steps can be slightly wider – even when you have a difficult letter.

# J-Words

**AJAR** – slightly open
**AJEE** – askew
**DOJO** – a room for martial arts
**FUJI** – Japanese cherry tree
**HAJI** – a visitor to Mecca
**KOJI** – a fungus
**MOJO** – a magical charm

**PUJA** – the act of worship
**RAJA** – an Indian king / prince

# Q-Words

**AQUA** – the color
**SUQS** – plural of **SUQ**, an Arabian market

# V-Words

Common V words: **EVEN, EVER, EVES, EVIL, OVAL, OVEN, OVER, OVUM;** then **CAVE, CAVY, COVE, DIVA, DIVE, DOVE, ENVY, FAVE, FIVE, GAVE, GIVE, HAVE, HIVE, HOVE, JIVE, LAVA, LIVE, LOVE, LUVS, NAVY, RAVE, REVS, ROVE, SAVE, WAVE, WAVY** and **WOVE.** More unusually…

**ARVO** – afternoon
**AVER** – assert
**AVOS** – Macao's monetary unit
**AVOW** – confess
**BEVY** – a large group
**DEVA** – devine beings
**EAVE** – where a roof meets a wall
**GYVE** – a shackle
**KAVA** – a shrub
**LAVE** – wash

**LEVA** – Bulgarian monetary unit

**LEVY** – tax

**NAVE** – main part of a church

**NEVE** – granular snow

**NEVI** – plural of **NEVUS**: birthmark

**RIVE** – tear apart

**TAVS / VAVS** – plurals of a Hebrew letter

**WIVE** – to marry

# X-Words

**AXED, AXES, AXIS, AXLE, EXAM, EXEC, EXIT, EXPO, OXEN** and **OXES**; then **BOXY, FOXY, NEXT, PIXY, SEXY, TAXI, TEXT, WAXY.** Here are some weirder words...

**AXIL** – botany term relating to the angle of leaves

**AXON** – nerve cell filament

**COXA** – hipbone

**DIXY** – large iron pot

**DOXY** – a lover

**EXES** – former partners

**EXON** – a **DNA** sequence

**EXPO** – exhibition

**FIXT** – fixed

**IXIA** – a South African iris

**LUXE** – expensive and desirable

**MIXT** – mixed

**MOXA** – substance used in eastern medicine

**OXID** – an oxygen compound

**SEXT** – church service

**TAXA** – groups of species, etc.

## Z-Words

**BOZO, BUZZ, COZY, DAZE, DOZE, DOZY, FAZE, FIZZ, FUZZ, GAZE, HAZE, HAZY, JAZZ, LAZE, LAZY, MAZE, OOZE, RAZE, SIZE.** And some more unusual words:

**ADZE** – axe-like tool

**AZAN** – a call to prayer

**COZE** – friendly chat

**CZAR / TZAR** – appointed leader

**FOZY** – spongy

**FUZE** – variant spelling of **FUSE**

**IZAR** – a long dress

**IZBA** – Russian log house

**MAZY** – maze like

**MOZO** – a male servant in Spain, etc.

**OOZY** – that which oozes

**ORZO** – a pasta

**OUZO** – a Greek liqueur
**SIZY** – viscous

# Letter Balance

Defined as 'the quality of deserving honor', **HONORIFICABILITUDINITATIBUS** is, at 26 letters, the longest word in the works of Shakespeare! It also has the delightful quality of perfectly alternating consonants and vowels throughout! If you play BANANAGRAMS a lot, though, you already know you're not guaranteed to pick up a consistently helpful balance of vowels and consonants. So as well as initially glancing around for word patterns and statistically likely words as you turn over your tiles, get a feeling for the vowel and consonant mix that you have. If you're heavy one way or the other, try to compensate for that in your first few moves.

# Getting Along with U and I

Multiple **U**'s and **I**'s can be a problem until you realize you can play any one of a few words and quickly rid yourself of them pretty much effortlessly:

**FILI** – an order of Irish poets
**IIWI** – a Hawaiian bird

**IWI** – in Māori, bones

**PIING** – to make into a pie

**UHURU** – the process by which a country becomes independent in Africa

**ULU** – a fish-scaling knife

**UMU** – another Māori word; an oven

**UTU** – yet another Māori word; it means reward

# Vowel-only Words

Ever heard of the word **EUOUAE**? No? Don't feel bad, hardly anyone has… It's a medieval musical cadence, used when singing the hymn *Gloria Patri*. Yes, really! It's noteworthy because it's a six-letter, all-vowel word – handy for BANANAGRAMS! Here's a selection of other vowel-only words:

**AA** – a volcanic lava

**AE** – one

**AI** – slow-moving, shaggy animal

**EA** – a river

**IO** – moth

**OI** – a moth; also a shout

**OU** – man

**AIA** – Eastern female servant

**AUA** – mullet

**AUE** – Māori exclamation

**EAU** – a river

**EUOI** – a cry of Bacchic frenzy

# Consonant-only Words

Having too many consonants can seem just as infuriating as having too few... But there are plenty of words to help you out of a tight spot. And always remember that while **TSK** is useful in its three-letter form, its doubling up is found in many dictionaries... Which makes the six-letter sound of disapproval **TSKTSK** a delight!

**BRR / BRRR** – the sound of shivering with cold

**BY** – next to

**BYS** – less important issues

**CRWTH** – an ancient stringed instrument

**CRY** – weep

**CRYPT** – burial vault

**CWM** – a circle / ring

**CWT** – a unit of weight

**CWTCH** – in Wales, U.K., a cuddle

**CYST** – an anatomical sac

**DRY** – free from moisture

**FLY** – travel through the air

**FLYBY** – a low-altitude flight

**FLYSCH** – type of marine rock

**FRY** – cook in hot oil

**FYRD** – the militia in Anglo-Saxon England

**GLYCYL** – pertaining to glycinic residue in protein

**GLYPH** – a picture / hieroglyph

**GRRL / GRRRL** – an aggressive girl

**GYM** – abbreviation of gymnasium

**GYMP** – material with wire running through it

**GYP** – to cheat

**GYPSY** – a nomadic person

**HM / HMM** – expression of thoughtfulness

**HWYL** – a Welsh word for an impassioned emotional quality

**HYMN** – a song praising God

**KYND** – variant spelling of **KIND**

**LYCH** – a dead body

**LYM** – a dog held on a cord

**LYMPH** – a fluid containing white blood cells

**LYNCH** – to put to death by hanging

**LYNX** – a wildcat

**MY** – of me

**MYRRH** – an aroma released by certain plants

**MYTH** – a legend

**NTH** – the last in a decreasing or increasing number

**NYMPH** – a female spirit

**NYS** – is not

**PFFT** – used to indicate dying / fizzling out

**PLY** – to work at diligently

**PRY** – an unwelcome enquiry

**PST** – sound used to attract attention

**PSYCH** – to psychologically intimidate

**PYGMY** – anything very small of its kind

**RYND** – a support in a millstone

**SCRY** – fortune telling with crystals

**SKYR** – in Iceland, a meal made from curdled milk

**SYND** – a sign that communicates information

**TRYP** – a parasitic life form

**TYPP** – a measurement in textiles

**TYPY** – a perfect specimen of an animal

**WYCH** – a salt pit

**WYND** – a narrow street

# SKIRL

Composing a theme song for his radio show, fictional psychiatrist Frasier Crane notes, "Nothing says despair so quickly as the skirl of a bagpipe…" to which his producer retorts: "Nothing says 'Turn off the radio' so quickly either!" But is **SKIRL** a real word? Indeed it is: a Scottish one that means 'a shrill cry'.

## "It's a Scottish word..."

Those four words continually fall from the author's lips as others question bizarre letter combinations in his grids... When people learn that these incredibly handy Scottish words really are in some dictionaries, they're genuinely stunned. Or **DONNERED** as they might say! Also, there are a few more Scottish entries in the 'three-letter words list' – see The Bit at the Back of the Book.

**AGIN** – against

**AULD** – old

**BAHOOKIE** – the buttocks

**BAIRN** – child

**BAWBEE** – an old coin

**BESOM** – a broom and, mockingly, a nagging partner!

**BRAW** – good

**BREEKS** – trousers

**CLAES** – clothes

**CLARTY** – sticky dirt

**DONNERED** – stunned

**DOWP** – your bottom

**DREEP** – dripping wet

**DUNT** – dull, hollow sound; a thud

**FANKLE** – a tangle

**GLAIKIT** – foolish

**GOWK** – the cuckoo bird; also a fool

**GUDDLE** – among other meanings, using the hands to catch fish

**HOLK** – to dig; also **HOWK**

**LANG** – long

**KEEK** – take a look

**MINGING** – foul smelling

**NEEP** – a turnip

**NEUK** – the corner of a building or street

**NYAFF** – a contemptible person or trivial object

**PIBROCH** – music for the bagpipes

**RAMMY** – a noisy brawl

**SCUNNER** – a strong dislike

**SEMMIT** – vest worn under a shirt

**SHOGGLE** – shake or dangle

**SKELLY** – squint

**SKIRL** – a shrill noise

**STOOK** – stack of corn or hay; straw, barley, etc.

**SYNE** – since

**THIRL** – a hole; the act of piercing something

**TREWS** – trousers

**WABBIT** – not what Elmer Fudd was hunting; it means tired

**WID** – with

**WIFIE** – a wife

If you think one or two of these words are familiar, you could be right. *Auld Lang Syne* is that poem people sing at New Year! It translates as 'old long since' but alludes to old time's sake. **LANG**'s worthy of particular mention, though, on account that as well as meaning 'long' in Scotland, it's also a way of making a wire rope that increases durability!

# Local Lexicons

It's not just Scotland that gives dictionaries unusual words of course. Our cousins in the U.K. have so many accents, dialects and quirky words that there are whole books dedicated to its regional languages. Here's a load of really handy letter combinations that are seldom heard outside small parts of Britain; words that even most Brits would be amazed to learn are in a dictionary.

**BOSTING** – superb (Midlands)

**CANK** – cackle like a goose, or gossip (all over)

**CERTY** – self-willed (Somerset)

**CHOCKER** – packed full (North-West)

**CHUMBLE** – to nibble or peck (Midlands)

**CLEM** – to feel the pinch of hunger (Midlands)

**CRWTH** – a crowd (Wales)

**CWM** – a valley formed by a glacier (Wales)

**CWTCH** – a cuddle; also a cupboard (Wales)

**DOTTLE** – plug of pipe tobacco (North-East; originally Scottish)

**GIMMEL** – narrow passage between houses (North-West)

**NESH** – soft; weak or feeling the cold (North-West)

**QUOB** – a bog – but also a throb (Cornwall; Isle of Wight)

**SLOOM** – a doze; light slumber (Cambridgeshire)

**SPELK** – a splinter or wooden splint (North-East)

**SQUINCH** – small crack between floorboards (Devon)

**WRASSE** – type of fish (Cornwall)

# The Antipodes

You may well have heard New Zealand and Australia referred to as 'The Antipodes' – defined as the other side of the world. The literal meaning, though, is 'opposite feet'! In any case, some dialect words from New Zealand and Australia are just **RIPPER**...

**ARVO** – afternoon (both)

**BOONIES** – middle of nowhere (both)

**CARK** – die (New Zealand)

**CHUR** – cheers; also goodbye (New Zealand)

**GIDDAY** – a salutation: 'good day' (both)

**JANDAL** – a flip flop (New Zealand)

**MOZZIE** – mosquito (both)

**MUNTED** – disastrously broken (New Zealand)

**PASH** – passionate kiss (New Zealand)

**RIPPER** – outstandingly good (Australia)

**SOOK** – young calf, or a shy / soft person (both)

**SQUIZ** – a quick glance (New Zealand)

# Rapid Peeling

Of all the ways to play BANANAGRAMS that cause fingers to wag, eyebrows to raise and tongues to cluck, this is the most divisive. Almost everyone who says they do it also says they feel guilty afterwards! So use it by all means, but don't say we didn't warn you...

## The Premise

Remember the Aesop's Fable that tells of an improbable race between a hare and a tortoise? Cocky and naturally swift, the hare races off at a considerable lick. Slow but intrepid, the tortoise follows. Alas, the hare, fatigued from his exertions, takes a nap before completing the course... And that proves to be his undoing. The tortoise's slow, steady pace wins the day: he overtakes the sleeping hare and is first to cross the finish line.

In real terms, imagine a player who, for a short time, calls **"PEEL"** again and again with great rapidity but fails to expand their two-letter efforts into words of three-or-more letters. Alternatively, perhaps that player slows to a crawl after each little flurry as they rearrange to avoid getting gridlocked...

# Be the Tortoise

Next imagine two opponents, subjected to a rapid volley of peels: each has a small backlog of tiles. It's very possible that they actually have a better selection of letters from which to make more advantageous words. Indeed, it's possible for a player who doesn't call **PEEL** for an entire hand to still win the game. Now – finally – imagine that this latter scenario isn't a chance occurrence but is, in fact, your strategy: for most of the game, you're going to be the tortoise!

In other words, only at a late moment during a game in which you have kept pace, you begin peeling and positioning letters so quickly that you simply swamp your competitors with new tiles. This moment comes at a time when there are few enough letters remaining that you can be sure your own grid will take the rapid influx.

# Rapid Peeling Secrets

For this strategy to work you have to focus on only one thing from the moment somebody says "**SPLIT**": keeping your grid in as versatile a form as possible. To that end, use everything you know only to keep up with other players. You must maintain your grid to the highest-possible standard. If you can lay your last tile and call **"PEEL"**, DON'T. Instead, put it down and keep improving your grid… Play using everything we're about to cover: 'Knowing The Moment', 'The Glisk' and 'Rapid Peeling Tips'.

# Knowing the Moment

The exact moment at which to begin Rapid Peeling varies from player to player and from hand to hand. It has to come with your own experience but, until you know what suits you, try allowing for at least five or six tiles per head… So in a two-player game there might be around ten or twelve tiles left in the **BUNCH**; in a game with three people perhaps 15 to 20.

# The Glisk

Defined as a fleeting glimpse, the word **GLISK** perfectly suggests the art of sneakily and hurriedly discerning two critical pieces of information in BANANAGRAMS. First, where other players are in their grid-building efforts. Second, the best moment to launch a volley of Rapid Peels.

As soon as you can, start developing the habit of glisking as you look up to **PEEL**. Rather than concerning yourself unduly with where in the **BUNCH** your hand is going, see instead what condition other people's grids are in and who is already backlogged. Especially concentrate on this when you're peeling tiles towards the end of the game.

## Rapid Peels

When you reach 'The Moment', you begin to **PEEL**... And you don't stop: it needs to be a smooth, relentless volley. If it helps, use alternate hands to pick up tiles: as one hand places a letter, the other reaches toward the **BUNCH** in readiness to take the next tile.

## Presume they're Backlogged

Don't bother to glisk the players anymore. Concentrate entirely on your tiles and your grid. Glance at new letters as you pick them up; drop your eyes down to look at your grid even while your hand is still moving back towards it. Keep rapidly peeling until the end of the game: remember, the idea is to simply swamp other players with the remaining tiles at such a rate that they can't concentrate enough to use the tile pool that's accumulating.

# Bananas!

Finally, if you had full confidence in your efforts prior to rapid peeling, don't bother to spell check at the end. Just call **"BANANAS!"** and get ready to handle the backlash if the other players realize what's happened!

# Rapid Peeling Tips

Here are some more hints, tips and techniques that are useful in any game, but particularly so when conditions are right for you to **PEEL** rapidly.

# Little Steps

The very old word **SCALARY** means, 'possessing the form of ladders or steps'. And, of course, you already know the advantages of playing your initial tile selection in a scalary fashion. Just as a big set of Steps is useful at the top end of the game, so too Little Steps come in handy when you want to **PEEL** rapidly toward the end.

Choose an area of your grid that lets you expand it quickly and extensively. If you're playing Steps, this may very well be the top-left or bottom-right corners and sides: most players tend to have more space there than bottom-left or top-right. Make sure you have a connecting word that takes you far enough out to play off, as in the picture on the right.

When you want to **PEEL** rapidly – or you find another player is peeling rapidly and you need to keep up – build a tiny set of steps using two or three-letter words in this area. Keep in mind that the letter **O** appears in more two-letter words than any other vowel, followed by **E** and then **I**. Be careful not to lock all your **O**'s in this area though – they have a higher purpose! We'll come back to that shortly.

# Grid Blind

Remember to stay calm if you're not able to get rid of some letters in your Little Steps; don't be 'grid blind'... You're still able to put them in other areas of your main grid. You just don't want to be clogging up the longer words in your grid with tiles if they can go somewhere out of the way.

# Two to Three and Three to Two

If you repeatedly take away one letter from the word **STARTLING** it creates a new word every time, **STARTING** with the removal of the **L**... Then goes a T: even as you're **STARING** at the word you might wonder: which letter is next to leave the **STRING**? Will you feel the **STING** of embarrassment if you can't guess, or proudly **SING** your own praises if you do? Be careful, though – pride is a deadly **SIN**! Now there are just two letters **IN** the word but the **N** comes away and leaves **I**... And when the **I** disappears, you're left with no letters at all!

This wordplay illustrates how words can break down and build up to a surprising degree. In a game of BANANAGRAMS, though, it's probably fair to say that the most useful skill is simply being able to turn two-letter words into words of three-or-more letters.

For that reason, this book first dealt with a list of two-letter words, then some lists of three that allow you to hurriedly play what many consider the trickiest letters – **J**, **Q**, **V**, **X** and **Z**. If you hope to commit anything to memory, then these are the most important: they improve your game immeasurably. Since one could argue, though, that Rapid Peeling depends greatly on your ability to change two-letter words to three-letter words, we'll soon give you an absolutely whopping list that lets you do just that. For now, though, we'll revisit some two-letter words that serve a special purpose…

# Docking Ports

It was the American founding father Benjamin Franklin that said it best: "If you fail to plan, you plan to fail!" Mind you, he also said, "Fart for freedom, fart for liberty, and fart proudly" so – you know – take his advice with a pinch of salt. And lavender. In any case, when you begin Rapid Peeling, you can build certain tiles in your grid to use as 'Docking Ports' ahead of their being needed. Here, we're going to give you the relevant words alongside the most useful 'Docking Ports'; the definitions appear from the next page onwards.

# Docking Port O's

As we mentioned earlier, **O** appears in more two-letter words than any other vowel. And happily, there are eleven **O**'s in the pouch! Even so, you really don't want to waste many by plonking them down willy-nilly or locking them up in the 'Little Steps' area. Instead, try and position a couple of **O**'s in places where you can play a tricky tile either side of them later in the game. The two-letter words that you can make with an **O** and one other letter are:

| | | | | |
|----|----|----|----|----|
| BO | LO | WO | OM | OW |
| DO | MO | YO | ON | OX |
| GO | NO | ZO | OO | OY |
| HO | OO | OB | OP | |
| IO | PO | OD | OR | |
| JO | SO | OF | OS | |
| KO | TO | OH | OU | |

# Docking Port I's

It's wise to keep at least a couple of **I**'s open for disposing of **Q**'s in the word **QI**. Take a look, too, at the advice we give under Hard **QIS** since this not only lets you cope with a **Q** but also prepares you to do away with at least one **Z**, possibly two. Plenty of other two-letter words can be made with an **I** and one other letter, of course:

| | | | | |
|----|----|----|----|----|
| AI | LI | SI | ID | IT |
| BI | MI | TI | IF | |
| DI | OI | XI | IN | |
| GI | PI | | IO | |
| HI | QI | | IS | |

# Docking Port EE

There's just something about the word **EYELEVEL** that we like! Maybe it's all those straight lines. Maybe it's that every other letter is a consonant... And maybe it's that the only vowel in it is an **E**. More interestingly, perhaps, there's a Scottish word that's made of just two E's: **EE**... It means an eye, with the plural being **EEN**. Among the common words you could make with an **EE** Docking Port are **BEE**, **DEE**, **FEE**, **GEE**, **NEE**, **PEE**, **SEE**, **TEE** and **WEE**.

You could also play **LEE** and **REE**: a side of something that's sheltered from the elements, and a walled enclosure respectively. Oh! And **EEK**, **EEL** and **EEN**.... The best reason to have a few double **EE** Docking Ports, though, is because it takes a **C** and three of the five tricky letters straight in front of it:

**CEE** – the letter **C**

**JEE** – alternative to **GEE**; as in "Jee whizz!"

**VEE** – the letter **V**

**ZEE** – American spelling of the letter **Z**

# E, I, E, I, O

With all these letters peppering your grid, parts of it might very well look like a song sheet for *Old MacDonald Had A Farm*! But just preparing a few **EE, I** and **O** Docking Ports can let you get rid of some very difficult tiles at great speed.

# Avoid Mistakes

Ever seen the old brainteaser that asks you to count how many times the letter **F** appears in the sentence, "Finished files are the result of years of scientific study combined with the experience of years"?

It seems that most people say three – but look again: there are actually six. For some reason many of us don't register the F's in the word 'of'! And given how easily one can overlook a specific letter – even when looking for it – you can probably imagine how many errors get missed when hurriedly building a word grid. So… Is there a way to reduce the number of mistakes you make as you play? In fact there are several!

# Keep Scanning

It's a lovely irony that one of the most misspelled words in our language is **MISSPELLED**! But because the words a player uses in BANANAGRAMS tend to be shorter rather than longer, the most common spelling errors are usually due to speed of play rather than ignorance. So as you lay your tiles, keep scanning your grid to make sure all your words are kosher! It's frustrating to discover a dodgy word as play continues, but it's far more frustrating to have another player discover one after you think you've won.

# Keep Your Letters Straight

One easily-avoided mistake that we occasionally see involves the higgledy-piggledy placement of tiles. No matter how rushed you are, be sure to play your words in straight lines. This way you avoid having an opponent find one word that runs into another and forms absolute gobbledegook.

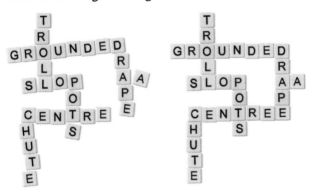

# Early Spell Check

If you're a fast player at the top end of the game then this advice is for you: after you've played your initial tiles – but before you call **"PEEL"** – take a moment. You might have between five and ten words that either form a sort-of staircase, or spur off that staircase. Here's the thing: there's a good chance that most of these words will be exactly the same at the end of the game as they are now – so quickly check their spelling before you call "**PEEL**".

# Late Spell Check

Similarly, if you're the kind of player that rapidly calls "**PEEL**", and consistently leaves other players with a backlog, you might also create a second opportunity to spell check. As the **BUNCH** depletes to only a handful of tiles, glance up at any other players' grids to see how many tiles 'behind' they are. If they have a fair few then you might find you can check your grid again before you call your next **PEEL** – or even just before you say "**BANANAS!**"

# Swiss Cheese Spell Check

Did you know that most Swiss cheese – the kind that's riddled with holes – is actually made in North America? And that the holes in these cheeses are known as 'eyes'? Indeed, Swiss cheese that's produced without holes is called 'blind'!

But what the devil has that got to do with spell-checking your grid? Well, if you're pushed for time, you can think of proofreading your grid as taste-testing Swiss cheese. Some bits are like the cheese – they need checking. Some bits are like the holes: they don't need checking...

For example, if you did a spell check of your Steps at the beginning, and haven't touched those words since, then skip them in your Late Spell Check. Likewise, if you had a spate of quick peels that went down cleanly in one part of the grid – as is often the case with Little Steps – again, skip it! Focus instead on the areas where you struggled terribly, played too quickly or made major changes.

# The Meaning of Ife

The speed of the game and the continual re-use of letters means that you'll sometimes end up with something that once was a word but now seems to be nothing of the kind. Maybe you had an **H** out of **HOWLING** and now have owling. Perhaps you grabbed a **G** from **GOOSE** and got oose. Or perchance you did exactly as one of the BANANAGRAMS team did in a very fast game: lost the **L** from **LIFE** leaving ife...

Well, before you despair in such situations it's well worth checking your dictionaries! Just because something doesn't look like a word, it doesn't mean it isn't. In these examples, **OWLING** is the act of smuggling sheep out of the U.K.*, **OOSE** is the name of the tiny fibres protruding from ropes or threads and, to the surprise of all, **IFE** is in some dictionaries as a tropical plant.

---

*Trust us, funny though that sounds, it's absolutely true!

# The Bit at the Back of the Book

"Some people have a way with words, and other people... Oh – uh – not have way." So says comedian, actor, musician and writer Steve Martin. He does have a way with words, of course! And here, in the much-trailed 'Bit at the Back of the Book', we'll offer up a word-related smorgasbord that shows why so many people who do have a way with words find them frolicsome, fun and fascinating.

To help with your BANANAGRAMS game there's a ready reckoner that – as promised – shows which of the two-letter words we gave you earlier can instantly convert to new words by adding one tile to their fronts or backs... There's also an absolutely enormous list that defines those three-letter words. And for those only just falling in love with language, we'll show a few of the ways that words can be playful! But first, the answer to what must be one of the questions we're asked most-often...

# Why are Some Words Words and Some Words Not Words?

**CORPUS**, Wurfing & **GLOSS**. Sounds exactly like the name of an accountancy firm, doesn't it? In fact, these three words are going to help answer that question... In short, what it really comes down to is somebody's best guess and personal taste.

## Wurfing

Even though they're from the same Roald Dahl book, **SCRUMDIDDLYUMPTIOUS** and 'snozzcumber' have different fates. **SCRUMDIDDLYUMPTIOUS** most definitely is in at least one dictionary – but we can't find 'snozzcumber' in any... And yet we know for a fact that snozzcumber very nearly was an entry! So too was the suggested noun 'wurfing', a proposed portmanteau word meaning to surf online while at work. To put that another way, **SCRUMDIDDLYUMPTIOUS** is playable, but 'snozzcumber' and 'wurfing' aren't – simply because none of the major dictionaries **GLOSSED** them...

# Glossed?

Yes, glossed! Ever wondered why a list of jargon at the back of a book is called a **GLOSSARY**? Well, the word comes from the verb **GLOSS** meaning to insert a word as an explanation. When dictionary editors put a new word in a dictionary, they say it's been glossed.

Glossing is complicated, though. Just for a moment, try to imagine the total number of words that are written in English – both online and off... And when we say words, we mean all words: medical terms, industry jargon, dialect phrases, spelling errors, slang, foreign words with no English equivalent, made-up-in-the-moment words... Think of even a fraction of what people write and you'll quickly appreciate that such a vast number of words could never really be glossed in a dictionary.

Consider too the short-lasting popularity of some words like the really awful **GRRRL** and you might even agree that not everything that could be glossed should be: editors need to choose carefully the locutions that forever earn a place in their dictionaries. And the simplest way to explain how they do it is to say that it relates to the frequency and duration of a word's use in everyday English... But how on earth do they measure these things? Why, with a corpus of course!

# Corpus

So what the heck is a corpus? In this context it's a formal term for a publisher's database of words. It's made up using software that analyzes the use of up to around 150 million words a month. New words – or new meanings for existing words – are considered by a team of editors who decide if the word has merit, will be around for a long time and is common enough to warrant an entry. In the end it's usually down to one person's best guess… And so we end up with surprising variation across dictionaries even though they all set out to do much the same thing. Snozzcumber just doesn't show up in everyday English enough to warrant an entry… **SCRUMDIDDLYUMPTIOUS** does. And as for wurfing? It's the first thing we look at in Some Ways to Play with Words.

# Some Ways to Play with Words

There are so many ways to play with words that it would take a book many times this size to catalog them. Here, though, are some of the most common and enduring…

# Portmanteau Words

We made mention of these earlier. In fact, a portmanteau was originally a travelling bag into which a great amount could be packed... But, typically offbeat, *Alice Through The Looking Glass* author Lewis Carroll had Humpty Dumpty use 'portmanteau' to describe "two meanings packed up into one word"... And now we have a lot of words that are just like that. Many of them are too transient to be glossed in dictionaries – but here are some that have been:

**BRUNCH** – breakfast and lunch

**CHILLAX** – chill and relax

**CHORTLE** – combination of chuckle and snort

**GLAMPING** – glamorous camping

**HANGRY** – a bit of a recent addition: angry because of hunger

**MIMSY** – miserable and flimsy; later delicate

**QUBIT** – useful word that combines quantum and bit

**SMOG** – smoke and fog

**SPORK** – combination of spoon and fork

**VLOG** – video and blog: **BLOG** itself is a portmanteau of **WEB** and **LOG**

# Anagrams

As you know, an anagram might best be described as a word or group of words that can be made into a new word or group of words by rearranging its letters. Our favorite example is **STIFLE** which is an anagram of **ITSELF**!

# Antigrams

When you rearrange some words, you discover they anagram in a way that means the new word somehow relates to the opposite of the original. Among the most delicious are...

**BUTCHERS** – cut herbs
**FORTY-FIVE** – over fifty
**FUNERAL** – real fun
**HONESTLY** – on the sly
**SILENT** – listen
**WITHIN EARSHOT** – I won't hear this

# Aptagrams

Just as an antigram carries a sense of opposition in itself, so too an aptagram rearranges in a way that feels entirely apt or relevant:

**A GENTLEMAN** – elegant man

**ELEVEN PLUS TWO** – twelve plus one

**MOON STARER** – astronomer

**NOTES** – tones

**SCHOOLMASTER** – the classroom

*IVANHOE* **by Sir Walter Scott** – a novel by a Scottish writer

Finally, Cory Calhoun made what is arguably the most fantastic of all the aptagrams we've ever seen... He takes a quote from Shakespeare's *Hamlet* and rearranges it to give you a summary of the whole darn play!

> "To be or not to be: that is the question, whether 'tis nobler in the mind to suffer the slings and arrows of outrageous fortune..."

> "In one of the Bard's best-thought-of tragedies, our insistent hero, Hamlet, queries on two fronts about how life turns rotten."

# Palindromes

Words that read the same backward as forwards must surely be among the earliest forms of word play that we discover as children. From **CIVIC** and **KAYAK** to **REDDER** and **RACECAR**, there are plenty of one-word palindromes.

Next there are the palindromes that use multiple words, and are palindromic in one of two ways: by word or by character. Examples of a sentence in which you can read each of the words backwards and still have the same sentence include this classic:

First ladies rule the State and state the rule: "ladies first".

Clearly, the words are in the same order, but the letters are not... That's the nature, though, of a character palindrome, among which some of the most delightful are, purely by coincidence, cat related:

Stack cats
Senile felines
Was it a car or a cat I saw?

Finally, the rhetorical question "I did, did I?" is an example of a sentence that is palindromic both by word and by character.

# Lipograms and Pangrams

This is fascinating! All of us at BANANAGRAMS HQ want to know how intriguing you'll find this notion: a paragraph of copy, or a chunk of writing, that works grammatically but omits a common factor... So what is it that turns this particular paragraph in to an illustration of how a lipogram works? Not only that but a pangrammatic lipogram for maximum impact. It looks plain. It sounds ordinary! And nothing's wrong with it as such; it's just a curious thing. Can you work out what's missing? You may look to no avail. Hint: think A to Z! Can you also draw a conclusion as to what a lipogram is? And a Pangram?*

# Steganography

While cryptography is the act of coding words or messages to ensure they can't be understood, steganography is the art of disguising a message so that it can't even be seen. For example, you could email someone a paragraph of text but have a second paragraph beneath it in a white font on the white background... You might also consider that elements of Dan Brown's *The Da Vinci Code* – and its prequels, sequels and equals – popularized the idea that Leonardo da Vinci hid messages in the images he painted.

---

*A pangram is a sentence or paragraph that includes every letter of the alphabet. The most well known is 'The quick brown fox jumps over the lazy dog'. A lipogram is a piece of text that omits one common letter. Finally, a pangrammatic lipogram is like our example – a piece of writing that contains every letter except one, in this case the most common: E.

# 12 Monkeys

Here's a steganography-type game... Throughout this book are 12 hidden mentions of monkeys, apes and ape-related words. Sure, we talk about them openly, but we mean properly hidden... How so? Well, in the course of telling you stuff, we split up some monkey words across a few other words...

For example, if we wanted to hide the word **MICE** we might do it as we did on page 29. The word **ICE** follows the letter **M** in 'firm', meaning that the word **MICE** is hiding right there in plain sight: fir**M ICE**. Now, our monkey / ape words might be spread across three or four words, and even have punctuation between them – but not other letters. Can you find them all?

| | |
|---|---|
| **MONKEY** | **PRIMATE** |
| **MANDRILL** | **HUMAN** |
| **GORILLA** | **GIBBON** |
| **APE** | **TARSIER** |
| **CHIMP** | **DARWIN** |
| **BABOON** | **GELADA** |

# Got Two – Now Add One

As you've heard throughout this book, a great knowledge of two-letter words can clearly make a difference in BANANAGRAMS… But you're probably finding that this alone isn't quite enough. You need more… That's because two-letter words don't give you enough options to play out from the grid and often seem hard to convert quickly. The solution to that is to know which of them can take a letter on their front or end to become a three-letter word without any rearrangement. Here's a chart that sums them all up…

| Letters to Play Before | Two Letter Words | Letters to Play After |
|---|---|---|
| B, M | AA | H, L |
| C, D, F, G, J, K, L, N, S, T, W | AB | A, S, Y |
| B, C, D, F, G, H, L, M, P, R, S, T, W | AD | D, O, S, Z |
| D, G, H, K, M, N, S, T, V, W | AE | |
| B, D, F, G, H, J, L, M, N, R, S, T, W, Y, Z | AG | A, E, O |
| A, B, D, F, H, L, N, P, R, Y | AH | A, I, S, U |
| R, T | AI | A, D, E, L, M, N, R, S, T |
| A, D, G, M, P, S | AL | A, B, E, L, P, S, T |
| B, C, D, G, H, J, L, N, P, R, S, T, Y | AM | A, I, P |
| B, C, D, E, F, G, H, M, N, P, R, S, T, V, W | AN | A, D, E, I, T, Y |
| B, C, E, F, G, J, L, M, O, P, T, V, W, Y | AR | B, C, E, F, K, M, S, T |
| B, E, F, G, H, K, L, M, P, R, V, W, Z | AS | H, K, P, S |

| | | |
|---|---|---|
| B, C, E, F, G, H, K, L, M, N, O, P, Q, R, S, T, V, W | AT | E, T |
| C, D, H, J, K, L, M, N, P, R, S, T, V, W, Y | AW | A, E, L, N |
| F, L, M, P, R, S, T, W, Z | AX | E |
| B, C, D, F, G, H, J, K, L, M, N, P, R, S, W, Y | AY | E, S |
| A, O | BA | A, D, G, H, M, N, O, P, R, S, T, Y |
| O | BE | D, E, G, L, N, T, Y |
| O | BI | B, D, G, N, O, S, T, Z |
| | BO | A, B, D, G, K, O, P, R, S, T, W, X, Y |
| A | BY | E |
| O | DA | B, D, E, G, H, K, L, M, N, P, W, Y |
| O | DE | B, E, F, I, L, N, V, W, Y |
| | DI | B, D, E, G, M, N, P, S, T, V |
| A, U | DO | B, C, E, G, H, L, M, N, O, R, S, T, W |
| K, L, P, S, T, Y, Z | EA | R, S, T |
| B, F, G, K, L, M, P, R, T, W, Z | ED | H, S |
| B, C, D, F, G, J, L, M, N, P, R, S, T, V, W, Z | EE | K, L, N |
| D, N, R | EF | F, S, T |
| F, H, M, P, Y | EH | S |
| B, C, D, E, G, M, S | EL | D, F, K, L, M |
| F, G, H, M, R | EM | E, S, U |
| B, D, E, F, G, H, K, M, P, S, T, W, Y | EN | D, G, S |
| F, H, P, S, Y | ER | A, E, G, K, N, R, S |
| H, O, P, R, T, Y | ES | E, S |
| D, H, K, L, R, S, V | EX | |
| | FA | B, D, G, H, N, R, S, T, X, Y |
| | FY | |
| | GI | B, D, E, G, N, P, S, T |
| A, E | GO | A, B, D, O, R, T, V, X |
| | GU | B, L, M, N, R, S, T, V, Y |

| | | |
|---|---|---|
| A, C, S, W | HA | D, E, G, H, J, M, N, O, P, S, T, V, W, Y |
| S, T | HE | H, M, N, P, R, S, T, W, X, Y |
| A, C, G, K, P | HI | C, D, E, M, N, P, S, T |
| O | HM | M |
| M, O, R, T, W, Z | HO | B, D, E, G, N, P, S, T, W, Y |
| A, B, D, F, G, H, K, L, M, R, V | ID | S |
| R | IF | F |
| A, B, D, F, G, H, J, K, L, P, R, S, T, W, Y, Z | IN | K, N, S |
| B | IO | N, S |
| A, B, C, D, G, H, K, L, M, P, Q, S, T, V, W, X | IS | H, M, O |
| A, B, C, D, F, G, H, K, L, N, P, R, S, T, W, Z | IT | A, S |
| | JA | B, G, K, M, P, R, W, Y |
| | JO | B, E, G, T, W, Y |
| O, S | KA | B, E, F, M, S, T, W, Y |
| S | KI | D, N, P, R, S, T |
| | KO | A, B, I, P, R, S |
| S | KY | E |
| A | LA | B, C, D, G, H, M, P, R, S, T, V, W, X, Y |
| | LI | B, D, E, N, P, S, T |
| C | LO | B, G, O, P, T, W, X |
| A | MA | A, C, D, E, G, L, N, P, R, S, T, W, X, Y |
| E, U | ME | D, E, G, H, L, M, N, S, T, W |
| A | MI | B, C, D, G, L, M, R, S, X |
| H, U | MM | |
| | MO | A, B, C, D, E, G, I, L, M, N, O, P, R, S, T, W |
| E | MU | D, G, M, N, S, T |
| A | NA | B, E, G, H, M, N, P, T, W, Y |
| A, O | NE | B, E, F, G, T, W |
| O | NO | B, D, G, H, N, O, R, S, T, W |
| G | NU | B, M, N, R, S, T |

**188**

| | | |
|---|---|---|
| B, C, D, F, G, H, J, K, L, M, N, R, S, Y | OB | A, E, I, S |
| B, C, G, H, M, N, P, R, S, T, Y | OD | A, D, E, S |
| D, F, H, J, M, R, T, V, W | OE | S |
| O | OF | F, T |
| D, F, N, O, P | OH | M, O, S |
| K, M, P | OI | K, L |
| D, M, R, S, T, V, Y | OM | S |
| C, D, E, F, H, I, M, N, S, T, W, Y | ON | E, O |
| B, C, D, G, L, M, N, P, R, T, W, Z | OO | F, H, P |
| B, C, F, H, K, L, M, O, P, S, T, W | OP | A, E, S, T |
| B, C, D, F, G, K, M, N, T, V | OR | A, B, C, E, T |
| B, C, D, H, I, K, M, N, P S, W, Z | OS | |
| F, S, Y | OU | D, R, T |
| B, C, D, H, J, L, M, N, P, R, S, T, V, W, Y | OW | E, L, N |
| B, C, F, G, L, P, S, V | OX | O, Y |
| B, C, F, H, J, S, T | OY | E, S |
| O, S | PA | C, D, H, L, M, N, P, R, S, T, W, X, Y |
| A, O | PE | A, C, D, E, G, H, N, P, R, S, T, W |
| | PI | A, C, E, G, N, P, R, S, T, U, X |
| | PO | D, H, I, L, O, P, S, T, W, X, Z |
| | QI | S |
| A, E, I, O | RE | B, C, D, E, F, G, I, M, P, S, T, V, X |
| A, I | SH | A, E, H, Y |
| P | SI | B, C, M, N, P, R, S, T, X |
| D, I | SO | B, C, D, L, M, N, P, S, T, U, W, X, Y |
| P | ST | Y |
| E, I, U | TA | B, D, E, G, I, J, M, N, O, P, R, T, U, V, W, X |

| | | |
|---|---|---|
| A, U | TE | A, D, E, G, N, S, T |
| | TI | C, E, L, N, P, S, T |
| | TO | D, E, G, M, N, O, P, R, T, W, Y |
| B, D, F, H, J, L, M, P, R, S, T, V, Y | UG | |
| D, H | UH | |
| B, G, H, L, M, N, R, S, T, V, Y | UM | E, M, P |
| B, D, F, G, H, J, M, N, P, R, S, T | UN | I, S |
| C, D, H, P, S, T, Y | UP | O, S |
| B, C, F, G, N, O, P | UR | B, D, E, N, P |
| B, G, J, M, N, P, S, W, Y | US | E |
| B, C, G, H, J, M, N, O, P, R, T | UT | A, E, S, U |
| A, E, O | WE | B, D, E, N, T, Y |
| T | WO | E, K, N, O, P, S, T, W |
| | XI | S |
| | XU | |
| P, R | YA | G, H, K, M, P, R, W, Y |
| A, B, D, E, K, L, N, P, R, T, W | YE | A, H, N, P, R, S, T, W |
| | YO | B, D, K, M, N, U, W |
| | YU | G, K, M, P, S |
| | ZA | G, P, S, X |
| A | ZO | A, O, S |

# Three-letter Definitions

Remember our defining the word **BOWDLERIZE** earlier? It means to sanitize a list or book by taking out rude or offensive words. We've done exactly that here, in just the same way as we're careful not to use certain words in certain company. So here are a lot of three-letter words that you can make just by adding a letter to the beginning or end of the two-letter words we listed earlier. Keep in mind that this isn't meant to be absolutely exhaustive and – again – we've put simple definitions for everything, even though you'll know some of the words.

**AAH** – exclamation
**AAL** – a shrub
**ABA** – a Syrian cloth
**ABS** – chest muscles
**ABY** – pay a penalty
**ADD** – combine
**ADO** – fuss
**ADS** – advertisements
**ADZ** – an axe-like tool
**AGA** – respectful title in the Ottoman Empire
**AGE** – get old
**AGO** – at a time in the past
**AHA** – exclamation of realisation
**AHI** – type of tuna
**AHS** – expressions of admiration
**AHU** – in Eastern Polynesia: a mound
**AIA** – female servants
**AID** – help
**AIE** – sound of alarm
**AIL** – sicken

**AIM** – purposee
**AIN** – Hebrew letter; Scottish word: own
**AIR** – oxygen
**AIS** – sloths
**AIT** – a small island
**ALA** – a wing-like structure
**ALB** – white robes of a priest
**ALE** – aloholic drink
**ALL** – everyone or everything
**ALP** – a tall mountain
**ALS** – shrubs
**ALT** – musical note
**AMA** – a Japanese woman diver
**AMI** – a friend, esp. a male
**AMP** – measure of current
**ANA** – collection of anecdotes
**AND** – also
**ANE** – Scottish word for 'one'
**ANI** – a tropical bird

ANT – insect
ANY – whichever
APE – type of primate
ARB – purchasing money for profitable reuse
ARC – part of a circle's curve
ARE – a measurement in the French metric system
ARF – a barking sound
ARK – a chest, box or type of boat
ARM – a limb
ARS – letter R's
ART – the expression of creativity
ASH – remnants of a fire
ASK – enquire
ASP – a snake
ASS – a donkey
ATE – past tense of eat
ATT – an old Siamese coin
AWA – old word for 'away'
AWE – sense of reverence
AWL – pointed tool for making holes
AWN – bristles on some grass types
AXE – a cutting tool

AYE – word meaning yes
AYS – yes votes
AZO – relates to specific ions / molecules
BAA – the noise made by a sheep or goat
BAD – not good
BAG – a carrying pouch
BAH – expression of contempt
BAM – loud noise
BAN – forbid
BAO – a steamed bun
BAP – a type of bread roll
BAR – a pub or drinking establishment
BAS – in Ancient Egypt, a person's spirit
BAT – visually-impaired mammal
BAY – land on the seafront
BED – furniture on which you sleep
BEE – the insect; also the letter B
BEG – plead
BEL – unit for measuring sound
BEN – a mountain

**BET** – the Hebrew letter

**BEY** – an official in the Ottoman Empire

**BIB** – hooting sound

**BID** – promise on money at auction

**BIG** – large

**BIN** – rubbish receptacle

**BIO** – biography

**BIS** – meaning 'twice', this is the word the French use for 'Encore'!

**BIT** – a small piece of something

**BIZ** – shortening of business; especially show biz

**BOA** – type of snake

**BOB** – move up and down as in water

**BOD** – a person

**BOG** – a quagmire

**BOK** – a goat

**BOO** – sound of disapproval

**BOP** – to dance; also the sound of being struck

**BOR** – shortening of neighbor

**BOS** – term for 'brothers'

**BOT** – the larva of the botfly

**BOW** – bend at the waist to take applause

**BOX** – container

**BOY** – young male

**BUG** – an unscientific name for insects

**BUM** – slang for the buttocks; also to borrow

**BUN** – bread roll

**BUR** – a prickly casing around some seeds

**BUS** – vehicle for public transport; omnibus

**BUT** – however

**BYE** – shortening of goodbye

**CAB** – taxi

**CAD** – a cheat or a scoundrel

**CAM** – disc that converts circular motion to linear

**CAN** – a tin for food

**CAR** – the vehicle

**CAT** – a mammal that owns its owners

**CAW** – sound of a crow, jackdaw, etc.

**CAY** – bank of sand and coral

**CEE** – the letter **C**

**CEL** – shortening of cellular phone

**CHA** – tea

**CHI** – an energy or life force

**CIS** – cisgender or cissexual

**CIT** – colloquial term for a citizen

**CLO** – unit expressing insulating properties

**COB** – a spider! Hence: cobweb

**COD** – type of fish

**CON** – a scam

**COO** – sound of a dove

**COP** – police officer

**COR** – expression of amazement

**COS** – type of lettuce

**COW** – bovine mammal

**COX** – one who instructs a team of rowers

**COY** – shy; modest

**COZ** – slang term for cousin

**CUP** – drinking vessel

**CUR** – mongrel dog

**CUT** – sever

**DAB** – daub

**DAD** – father

**DAE** – Scottish word for 'do'

**DAG** – to cut away matted wool or fur

**DAH** – the longer tone (the dash) in Morse Code

**DAK** – a transport system for people or post

**DAL** – A measure of liquid

**DAM** – structure that holds back water

**DAN** – marker buoy at sea

**DAP** – to take part in a type of flyfishing

**DAW** – shortening of jackdaw

**DAY** – a period of 24 hours

**DEB** – shortening of debutante: a female socialite

**DEE** – the letter **D**

**DEF** – very good

**DEI** – god

**DEL** – differential operator

**DEN** – the lair of some animals

**DEV** – a good spirit

**DEW** – moisture droplets on the ground

**DEY** – a servant

**DIB** – a type of fishing

**DID** – past tense of do

**DIE** – cease to exist

**DIG** – burrow into

**DIM** – not bright

**DIN** – a word for a ghastly noise

**DIP** – momentarily submerge in liquid

**DIS** – to show disrespect

**DIT** – the shorter tone in Morse Code

**DIV** – a foolish person

**DOB** – to inform on

**DOC** – shortening of doctor

**DOE** – female rabbit, deer, etc.

**DOG** – domesticated canine

**DOH** – a musical note

**DOL** – unit of measurement of pain

**DOM** – a monk's title

**DON** – to dress or put on

**DOO** – Scottish word for a dove

**DOR** – some species of insect

**DOS** – slang word for parties or events

**DOT** – a small, circular mark

**DOW** – to prosper

**DSO** – variant spelling of ZO

**DUG** – past tense of dig

**DUH** – sarcastic expression highlighting obviousness

**DUN** – repeatedly make demands of another

**DUP** – to open

**DYE** – change the colour of material

**EAN** – give birth

**EAR** – the organ through which you hear

**EAS** – rivers

**EAT** – consume food

**ECO** – an environmental activist

**EDH** – a character in the runic alphabet

**EDS** – educations

**EEK** – sound of a small shriek or squeak

**EEL** – long fish

**EEN** – Scottish word for eyes

**EFF** – the letter F

**EFS** – more than one letter F

**EFT** – a newt

**EGO** – one's self image

**EHS** – exclamations of surprise

**ELD** – old age

**ELF** – person of diminutive size that helps Santa

**ELK** – a large deer

**ELL** – a very old unit of measure

**ELM** – type of tree

**EME** – Scottish word for an uncle or friend

**EMS** – letter Ms

**EMU** – large flightless bird

**END** – finish

**ENG** – ŋ symbol in dictionary pronunciation alphabets

**ENS** – letter Ns

**EON** – a long period of time

**ERA** – a period in time

**ERE** – before, in time

**ERG** – unit of energy or work

**ERK** – exclamation of dismay

**ERN** – sea eagle

**ERR** – make an error

**ERS** – a type of plant

**ESE** – form of address for a man

**ESS** – the letter S

**ETA** – Greek letter

**ETH** – Runic letter; EDH

**EWE** – female sheep

**EYE** – the organ that sees

**FAB** – shortening of fabulous

**FAD** – trend

**FAG** – U.K. slang for a cigarette

**FAH** – musical note

**FAN** – ardent admirer

**FAR** – distant

**FAS** – musical notes

**FAT** – overweight

**FAX** – telecommunications machine

**FAY** – fairy

FED – past tense of feed

FEE – sum of money paid for service

FEH – exclamation of disgust

FEM – shortening of feminine

FEN – boggy lowland

FID – tool for separating rope to be spliced

FIN – appendage on a fish

FIT – healthy

FOB – a watch chain

FOE – enemy

FOH – exclamation of disgust

FON – to compel

FOP – a dandy dresser

FOR – in support of

FOU – bushel

FOX – canine mammal said to be cunning

FOY – loyalty

FUG – stuffy atmosphere

FUN – enjoyment

FUR – hair of an animal

GAB – talk, especially rapidly or persuasively

GAD – travel in search of fun

GAE – Scottish word: GO

GAG – a joke

GAL – female

GAM – a school of whales

GAN – go

GAR – type of fish; GARPIKE

GAS – not solid, not liquid

GAT – a pistol

GAY – attracted to person of same sex

GED – Scottish word for a type of fish; the PIKE

GEE – exclamation of excitement

GEL – a dandy little word for any jelly-like material

GEM – any valuable stone

GEN – gain information

GHI – a type of butter used in Indian cooking

GIB – GIBBON definition from LB

GID – disease among sheep

**GIE** – Scottish word for **GIVE**

**GIG** – a show especially one by a musician / comedian

**GIN** – an alcoholic drink

**GIP** – to vomit

**GIS** – suits worn in martial arts

**GIT** – person for whom you have only contempt

**GNU** – type of antelope

**GOA** – a Tibetan gazelle

**GOB** – a mouth, particularly a big one

**GOD** – deity

**GOO** – slime

**GOR** – a seagull

**GOT** – acquired

**GOV** – shortened form of governor

**GOX** – gaseous oxygen

**GUB** – hit someone in the mouth

**GUL** – design used in oriental carpets

**GUM** – the part of the mouth that holds in your teeth

**GUN** – a weapon

**GUR** – unrefined cane sugar

**GUS** – musical instruments; like lutes

**GUT** – stomach

**GUV** – shortened form of governor

**GUY** – a man

**HAD** – owned or possessed

**HAE** – Scottish word for have

**HAG** – a crone of a woman

**HAH** – exclamation of triumph or derision

**HAJ** – a pilgrimage to Mecca; also **HADJ**

**HAM** – meat from a pig

**HAN** – had

**HAO** – Vietnamese currency

**HAP** – luck – hence: **HAPLESS**

**HAS** – possesses

**HAT** – headwear

**HAV** – haversine: a function in maths

**HAW** – berry of the hawthorn

**HAY** – food for livestock

**HEH** – exclamation of suspicion or satisfaction

**HEM** – finished edge of a fabric

**HEN** – female chicken

**HEP** – cheerleading exclamation: hep, hep... Hooray!

**HER** – that female

**HES** – plural of **HE**

**HET** – Scottish word for **HOT**

**HEW** – chop with an axe

**HEX** – curse

**HEY** – exclamation to gain attention

**HIC** – involuntary sound of a **HICCUP** or **HICCOUGH**

**HID** – concealed

**HIE** – hurry

**HIM** – that man

**HIN** – Hebrew measure of liquid capacity

**HIP** – the bone than connects your leg to your torso

**HIS** – belonging to him

**HIT** – strike

**HMM** – exclamation of acknowledgement / consideration

**HOB** – flat part of cooker

**HOD** – equipment for carrying bricks

**HOE** – tool for breaking up soil

**HOG** – pig

**HON** – shortened form of 'honey'; used affectionately

**HOP** – short jump; jump up and down on one leg

**HOS** – plural of HO: cessation; moderation

**HOT** – of a high temperature

**HOW** – means by which

**HOY** – exclamation to gain attention

**HUG** – a cuddle

**HUH** – exclamation of enquiry

**HUM** – an aroma; usually unpleasant

**HUN** – shortened form of 'honey'; used affectionately

**HUP** – exclamation to gee along a horse

**HUT** – wooden outbuilding

**IDS** – plural of **ID**: the unconscious mind

**IFF** – in logic, a shortening of 'If and only if'

**INK** – pigment used to write

**INN** – hotel

**INS** – ways to approach companies or people

**ION** – an atom charged with electricity

**IOS** – exclamations of triumph

**IRE** – wrath; anger

**ISH** – in part: 'It was true… Ish.'

**ISM** – a belief, view or system

**ISO** – very short segment of film

**ITA** – type of palm tree

**ITS** – possessive form of **IT**

**JAB** – prod

**JAG** – a rough edge

**JAK** – variant spelling of **JACK**; a lifting tool

**JAM** – preserve for toast and sandwiches

**JAP** – splash

**JAR** – vessel for liquids

**JAW** – bone attaching to the skull

**JAY** – type of bird

**JEE** – exclamation of surprise; also **GEE**

**JIN** – evil spirit

**JOB** – occupation

**JOE** – coffee

**JOG** – an exercise; worse than walking better than running

**JOT** – note down hurriedly

**JOW** – to ring, as with a bell

**JOY** – feeling of great happiness

**JUG** – vessel to serve liquids

**JUN** – monetary unit in North and South Korea; **CHON**

**JUS** – thin gravy. Also, power. Don't confuse the two

**JUT** – poke out

**KAB** – alternative spelling of **CAB**

**KAE** – a jackdaw

**KAF** – 22nd letter in Hebrew alphabet

**KAS** – spirits in Ancient Egypt

**KAT** – alternative spelling of **QAT** – a shrub

**KAW** – alternative spelling of **CAW** – noise of a crow

**KAY** – the letter **K**

**KEA** – type of parrot

**KED** – a parasitic louse

**KEN** – knowledge

**KEX** – type of plant

**KHI** – 22nd letter in Greek alphabet

**KID** – human child or young goat

**KIN** – blood relatives

**KIP** – a short sleep

**KIR** – alcoholic drink

**KIS** – plural of **KI**; a life force

**KIT** – equipment

**KOA** – type of tree

**KOB** – type of antelope

**KOI** – type of fish

**KOP** – a hill

**KOR** – Hebrew unit of liquid capacity

**KOS** – a unit of distance used in India

**KYE** – fundraising meeting in Korea

**LAB** – shortened form of **LABORATORY**

**LAC** – 100,000 rupees; also **LAKH**

**LAD** – young man

**LAG** – fall behind as when racing, etc.

**LAH** – musical note

**LAM** – aggressive attack

**LAP** – the front of your upper thighs when sitting

**LAR** – young man

**LAS** – musical notes

**LAT** – muscle

**LAV** – shortened form of **LAVATORY**

**LAW** – rules set by the start

**LAX** – undisciplined

**LAY** – lie down

**LEA** – meadow

**LED** – directed

**LEE** – sheltered side of a mountain, building, etc.

**LEX** – a body of laws

**LIB** – to castrate

**LID** – cover for a container or vessel

**LIE** – a falsehood

**LIN** – cease

**LIP** – the part of the mouth that needs licking

**LIS** – a circular enclosure

**LIT** – illuminated

**LOB** – throw

**LOG** – piece of tree trunk

**LOO** – toilet

**LOP** – cut off

**LOT** – a large number of people, objects, etc.

**LOW** – not high

**LOX** – type of smoked salmon

**LUG** – carry awkwardly or effortfully

**LUM** – Scottish word for a chimney

**LYE** – a caustic solution used for cleaning

**MAA** – a bleating sound, especially of a goat

**MAC** – short form of macintosh: a raincoat

**MAD** – insane

**MAE** – Scottish word for more

**MAG** – short form of magazine. Also, to chat

**MAL** – disease

**MAN** – male human

**MAP** – representation of an area for navigation

**MAR** – spoil

**MAS** – mothers

**MAT** – fabric area that partly covers floors

**MAW** – the mouth, throat and stomach of an animal

**MAX** – the greatest amount

**MAY** – perhaps

**MED** – doctor

**MEE** – type of noodle

**MEG** – shortened form of **MEGABYTE**

**MEH** – exclamation of indifference

**MEL** – in medicine **MEL** is used: a given name for honey

**MEM** – 13th letter of the Hebrew alphabet

**MEN** – males of the human race

**MES** – musical notes

**MET** – past tense of **MEET**

**MEW** – sound made by a cat

**MHO** – old unit of electrical conductance

**MIB** – a marble in a game; also **MIG**

**MIC** – shortened form of **MICROPHONE**

**MID** – among

**MIG** – a marble in a game; also **MIB**

**MIL** – unit of length: 1000th of an inch

**MIM** – prim; a term also for affected modesty

**MIR** – formerly a Russian commune

**MIS** – musical notes

**MIX** – merge things together; shuffle

**MOA** – extinct bird

**MOB** – an unruly crowd

**MOC** – short form of **MOCCASIN**

**MOD** – in the U.K. of the 1960s, a youth subculture

**MOE** – more

**MOG** – U.K. term for an unremarkable cat; also **MOGGIE**

**MOI** – me: often used when feigning innocence

**MOL** – the **SI** amount / unit **MOLE**

**MOM** – mother

**MON** – dialect spelling on **MAN**

**MOO** – sound made by cows

**MOP** – equipment with which to clean hard floors

**MOR** – humus

**MOS** – moments

**MOT** – a young woman

**MOW** – act of cutting grass

**MUD** – sodden earth

**MUG** – vessel for hot drinks

**MUM** – mother

**MUN** – like **MAUN**, a dialect word for **MUST**

**MUS** – plural of **MU**: a Greek letter

**MUT** – a dog without pedigree; a **MUTT**

**NAB** – to steal quickly; also to arrest someone

**NAE** – Scottish word for **NO**

**NAG** – to badger another person

**NAH** – exclamation of disinterest or the negative; **NO**

**NAM** – seize property as payment of debt

**NAN** – one of your parents' mothers

**NAP** – a short sleep

**NAT** – one who supports nationalism

**NAW** – no

**NAY** – no; especially a no vote

**NEB** – beak of a bird

**NEE** – formerly known as

**NEF** – long aisle in the centre of a church

**NEG** – photographic negative

**NET** – fabric made from mesh

**NEW** – recently produced

**NIT** – a louse's egg or larva

**NOB** – elite member of society

**NOD** – move the head affirmatively

**NOG** – drink made with beaten eggs

**NOH** – Japanese drama

**NON** – not

**NOO** – a Japanese drama

**NOR** – not this either

**NOS** – plural of **NO**

**NOT** – expressing denial and negation

**NOW** – in the present; immediately

**NUB** – the heart of the matter; the point

**NUM** – sound of eating: **YUM**

**NUN** – female member of religious order

**NUR** – a knot in wood; also **KNUR** and **KNURL**

**NUS** – plural of **NU**; a Greek letter

**NUT** – seed in a fruit with a hard shell

**NYE** – a brood of pheasants

**OAR** – propelling tool for a boat

**OAT** – a grain

**OBA** – a ruler in West Africa

**OBE** – ancient Laconian village

**OBI** – sash tied round waist

**OBS** – objections; expressions of opposition

**ODA** – a room in a harem

**ODD** – unusual

**ODE** – poem

**ODS** – mysterious energies

**OES** – Scottish word for grandchildren

**OFF** – not on

**OFT** – often

**OHM** – unit of electrical resistance

**OHO** – exclamation of surprise

**OHS** – exclamations of surprise

**OIK** – unruly person

**OIL** – liquid used for fuel and lubrication

**OKA** – in Turkey, a unit of weight

**OMS** – mantric words

**ONE** – single unit

**ONO** – type of fish

**OOF** – exclamation of pain or horror

**OOH** – exclamation of intrigue

**OOP** – Scottish word meaning to tie

**OPA** – a grandfather

**OPE** – open

**OPS** – operations

**OPT** – choose

**ORA** – plural of **OS**; an orifice

**ORB** – globe

**ORC** – type of whale

**ORE** – rock with metal in it

**ORT** – a scrap of leftover food

**OUD** – a musical instrument

**OUR** – belonging to you and me

**OUT** – not in

**OWE** – be in debt

**OWL** – a type of bird

**OWN** – possess

**OXO** – a link comprising one oxygen atom between two other atoms

**OXY** – containing oxygen atoms

**OYE** – a grandchild

**OYS** – grandchildren

**PAC** – a soft shoe

**PAD** – cushion

**PAH** – exclamation of contempt

**PAL** – friend

**PAM** – in a pack of cards, the jack of clubs

**PAN** – cooking utensil

**PAP** – soft, easy to digest food

**PAR** – average condition

**PAS** – fathers

**PAT** – tap gently

**PAW** – cushioned foot of dogs, cats, etc.

**PAX** – Latin for **PEACE**

**PAY** – remunerate

**PEA** – the vegetable

**PEC** – chest muscle

**PED** – a pannier

**PEE** – urinate

**PEG** – clip or restraining pin

**PEH** – Hebrew letters

**PEN** – writing implement

**PEP** – energy

**PER** – for each

**PES** – an animal's foot

**PET** – animal kept for companionship

**PEW** – seat in church

**PHI** – 21st letter of Greek alphabet

**PIA** – a herb

**PIC** – photograph

**PIE** – pastry–based dessert

**PIG** – the animal

**PIN** – pointed metal rod for joining things

**PIP** – seed in fruit

**PIR** – Sufi master

**PIS** – plural of **PI**; Greek letter

**PIT** – hole in the ground

**PIU** – more; as in more clear, more sure

**PIX** – short form of pictures

**POD** – case for seeds, etc.

**POH** – exclamation of disgust

**POI** – ball on a string used in dances

**POL** – a political campaigner

**POO** – polite word for excrement

**POP** – short, hollow high-pitch sound

**POS** – chamber pots

**POT** – round, deep container

**POW** – short but loud explosive sound

**POX** – disease that causes pustules

**POZ** – short and ghastly form of **POSITIVE!**

**PSI** – 23rd letter of the Greek alphabet

**PST** – sound one makes to discreetly get attention

**PUG** – type of dog

**PUN** – play on words

**PUP** – young dog

**PUR** – sound a contented cat makes; also **PURR**

**PUS** – yellow-white fluid in infected tissue

**PUT** – place

**PYA** – a coin in Burma

**PYE** – alternative spelling of **PIE**

**QAT** – a shrub; also **KHAT** and **KAT**

**QIS** – plural of **QI**: an energy

**RAD** – shortened form of **RADICAL**, meaning great

**RAG** – scrap of cloth

**RAH** – U.S. word for **CHEER**

**RAI** – in Algeria, a type of music

**RAM** – a male sheep

**RAN** – past tense of **RUN**

**RAS** – headland

**RAT** – a rodent

**RAW** – uncooked

**RAX** – stretch out

**RAY** – a beam such as with light

**REB** – U.S. word for a Confederate soldier

**REC** – short form of **RECREATION**

**RED** – the colour

**REE** – Scottish word for a walled enclosure

**REF** – short form of **REFEREE**

**REG** – a desert ground characterised by rock and stone

**REI** – an old Portuguese coin

**REM** – ionising radiation

**REP** – short form of **REPRESENTATIVE**

**RES** – short form of **RESIDENTIAL**

**RET** – moisten material such as flax, hemp, etc.

**REV** – short form of **REVOLUTION**

**REX** – Latin for king

**RHO** – 17th letter in the Greek alphabet

**RID** – free from

**RIF** – lay off

**RIN** – Japanese monetary unit

**RIT** – Scottish word for a cut, slash or slit

**ROB** – steal

**ROD** – pole

**ROE** – fish eggs

**ROM** – a male Romany Gypsy

**ROO** – baby kangaroo

**ROW** – straight line, especially a horizontal one

**RUG** – decorative fabric that partly covers floors

**RUM** – alcoholic drink

**RUN** – to move more quickly than walking

**RUT** – narrow trench, especially one made by a wheel

**RYA** – type of rug

**RYE** – an edible grain

**SAB** – short form of **SABOTEUR**

**SAD** – unhappy

**SAE** – Scottish word for **SO**

**SAG** – to sink in the centre

**SAL** – salt!

**SAM** – part of the leather making process

**SAN** – short form of **SANITARIUM**

**SAT** – past tense of sit

**SAW** – past tense of see

**SAX** – short form of **SAXOPHONE**

**SAY** – speak, or express through writing

**SEA** – watery mass full of fish and plastic beads

**SEE** – observe with the eyes

**SEL** – Scottish word for **SELF**

**SEN** – monetary unit in numerous countries

**SER** – a unit of weight used in India

**SEX** – gender identity

**SHA** – exclamation meaning "Be quiet!"

**SHE** – that woman

**SHH** – exclamation meaning "Be quiet!"

**SHY** – not outgoing; introverted

**SIB** – short for **SIBLING**: their kids are your **NIBLINGS!**

**SIC** – Latin for **THUS**

**SIM** – any computer game that simulates activities

**SIN** – a transgression against a god

**SIP** – drink a very small amount

**SIR** – firm of address for men

**SIS** – short form of **SISTER**

**SIT** – rest on one's backside

**SIX** – number that follows five and precedes seven

**SKA** – style of music

**SKI** – runner on foot for moving downhill on snow

**SKY** – upper atmosphere

**SOB** – cry noisily as when having to define thousands of words

**SOC** – local right of jurisdiction

**SOD** – grass and earth; turf

**SOL** – old Peruvian currency

**SOM** – currency in Kyrgyzstan and Uzbekistan

**SON** – a human's male offspring

**SOP** – absorb liquid; sometimes a word for a drunkard

**SOS** – musical notes

**SOT** – a drunkard

**SOU** – an old French coin

**SOW** – a female pig

**SOX**\* – socks!

**SOY** – dark sauce often used in oriental cooking

**SPA** – a mineral spring said to bring good health

**STY** – the home of a pig

**SUG** – sell under the guise of conducting research

**SUM** – a mathematical problem

**SUN** – heat-giving star

**SUP** – drink minutely; as with **SIP**

**SUS** – short form of **SUSS**: to see through or work out

**TAB** – flap

**TAD** – a small amount

**TAE** – Scottish word for **TOE**

**TAG** – a label

**TAI** – type of fish

**TAJ** – type of hat in Muslim countries

**TAM** – tam-o'-shanter' a type of Scottish hat

**TAN** – the color

**TAO** – in some philosophies, "the right path"

**TAP** – sound of a gentle knock

**TAR** – sticky black goo; asphalt / bitumen

**TAT** – tatty objects

**TAU** – 19th letter of Greek alphabet

**TAV** – last letter of Hebrew alphabet

**TAW** – a process in leather making

**TAX** – the government's share of your earnings

**TEA** – leaves used to make a hot drink

**TED** – to dry hay

---

\*If you spell **SOCKS** out loud, it sounds as if you're saying the Spanish phrase ¡Eso sí que es! meaning, roughly "That's what it is!"

**TEE** – pointed 'cup' on which a golf ball rests

**TEG** – a sheep in its second year

**TEN** – number following nine and preceding eleven

**TES** – musical notes

**TET** – ninth letter of Hebrew alphabet; **TETH**

**THE** – definite article

**THO** – short form of **THOUGH**

**TIC** – involuntary muscular twitch

**TIE** – bind

**TIL** – the sesame plant

**TIN** – a metal

**TIP** – lift by one side

**TIS** – musical notes

**TIT** – type of bird

**TOD** – measure of weight; especially for wool

**TOE** – a digit on your foot

**TOG** – the measure of the insulation of a duvet

**TOM** – male turkey or cat

**TON** – a weight

**TOO** – also

**TOP** – uppermost part or surface

**TOR** – a hill

**TOT** – young child

**TOW** – pull along behind

**TOY** – plaything

**TUG** – pull sharply and quickly

**TUM** – the stomach

**TUN** – a barrel for beer

**TUP** – a ram

**TUT** – exclamation indicating mild irritation

**TWO** – number following one and preceding three

**TYE** – a sorting trough in mining

**UDO** – a herb

**UME** – an Asian tree

**UMM** – exclamation indicating hesitation

**UMP** – short form of **UMPIRE**

**UNI** – short form of **UNIVERSITY**

**UNS** – 'ones'; "the young uns play faster than me."

**UPO** – upon

**UPS** – upward movements: more ups than downs

**URB** – short form of **URBAN**

**URD** – type of plant

**URE** – **AUROCHS**: ox extinct since 1627. Also **URUS**

**URN** – a storage vessel much like a vase

**URP** – onomatopoeic word for vomiting

**USE** – employ

**UTA** – type of lizard

**UTE** – short form of **UTILITY**

**UTS** – musical notes

**UTU** – a reward

**VAE** – humiliation of a defeated party

**VAN** – vehicle

**VAR** – alternating currents: unit of reactive power

**VAS** – a vessel or duct

**VAT** – large container for liquids

**VAW** – Hebrew letter

**VEE** – the letter V

**VEX** – annoy

**VID** – short form of **VIDEO**

**VIS** – power or force

**VOE** – a creek or bay

**VOM** – vomit

**VOR** – warn

**VOW** – oath

**VOX** – Latin for **VOICE**

**VUG** – a crack or cavity in rocks

**VUM** – swear

**WAB** – web

**WAD** – thick quantity of things

**WAE** – woe

**WAG** – shake from side to side, as with a dog's tail

**WAN** – unhealthily pale

**WAR** – conflict

**WAS** – that which has been

**WAT** – wet

**WAW** – sixth Hebrew letter; also **VAV**

**WAX** – substance used to make candles

**WAY** – means by which

**WEB** – pattern woven by spiders, for example

WED – marry

WEE – urinate

WEN – a type of cyst

WET – not dry!

WEY – appropriately enough, a unit of weight

WHA – Scottish word for WHO

WHO – which person?

WIN – succeed; triumph – beat others at BANANAGRAMS

WIS – to suppose something, or to know it

WIT – clever, personable, humor

WOE – grief

WOK – wide, open cooking pan

WON – past tense of win

WOO – to encourage the love of another

WOP – chopping or beating action / sound; also WHOP

WOS – plural of WO; an alternative to WOE

WOT – to know

WOW – exclamation of amazement

WUS – a form of somewhat affectionate address

WYE – the letter WYE

XIS – plural of XI; 14th letter of Greek alphabet

YAG – an artificial crystal

YAH – exclamation of agreement, or "yes"

YAK – scruffy–looking ox

YAM – a root vegetable

YAP – an onomatopoeic word: short, high-pitch noise

YAR – nimble; swift

YAW – the sideways turning of ships and planes

YAY – the noise of a cheer

YEA – yes

YEH – yes

YEN – Japanese currency

YEP – yes

YER – your

YES – affirmative

**YET** – as of now

**YEW** – type of tree

**YIN** – Scottish word for 'one'

**YOB** – a ne'er do well; a hooligan

**YOD** – tenth letter in the Hebrew alphabet

**YOK** – a satisfied chuckle; also **YUK**

**YOM** – day

**YON** – those over there

**YOU** – a person being addressed

**YOW** – exclamation of pain; a howl

**YUG** – one of four ages of mankind in Hindu cosmology

**YUK** – a satisfied chuckle; also **YOK**

**YUM** – exclamation of enjoyment when eating

**YUP** – yet another word for "yes"

**YUS** – one more word for **YES**

**ZAG** – to move to one side sharply

**ZAP** – energy; vim

**ZAS** – plural of **ZA** – short form of **PIZZA**

**ZAX** – an ax-like tool

**ZEA** – a type of plant

**ZED** – in the U.K., the letter **Z**

**ZEE** – in the U.S., the letter **Z**

**ZHO** – variant spelling of **ZO**, a yak / cattle hybrid

**ZIN** – a type of tree

**ZIT** – a spot or boil

**ZOA** – onomatopoeic; the same as **ZOOM**

**ZOO** – a place where animals are shown in captivity

**ZOS** – plural of **ZO**: a yak / cattle hybrid

# All's Well that Ends Well...

And, indeed, our revels now are ended! Tragedy though that is, we hope you continue dipping into the many Sneaky Tips in *The Little Book of BANANAGRAMS*... As well as words, clogs, bananas and anagrams, we've touched on yaks, goats, monkeys and Shakespeare. Ah, Shakespeare... His 'Yaks Go Mad' Sonnet is a classic. We've made that up, of course – 'Yaks Go Mad Sonnet' is an anagram of "Goats and Monkeys", which is something Othello exclaims in Act 4, Scene 1 of the eponymous tragedy...

Interestingly, the word **TRAGEDY** originally meant 'song of a goat' – **GOAT** is an anagram of **TOGA**. A toga is worn in several Shakespearian tragedies. Shakespeare's best known tragedy is **HAMLET**. Hamlet is an anagram of Thelma. Thelma Houston sang 'Don't Leave Me This Way' and gyrated to the hot soul anthem! '**HOT SOUL ANTHEM**' is an anagram of Thelma Houston, and **GYRATED** is an anagram of **TRAGEDY**! Coincidence? Yes. Truth be told, we only mentioned all this because we were 181 words short – not counting the acknowledgements and 'Last Word', which follow...

# The Last Word

The last word in a number of dictionaries is the name of a genus of a long-snouted weevil, 'Zyzzyva'. That's not our last word, though, because – with only two **Z**'s in the classic BANANAGRAMS – you can't play it!

Instead, we end with an archaic four-letter word that distinguishes itself in two ways… First, it contains no major vowels. Second, it begins with the last three letters of the alphabet in reverse order. Unfortunately, its meaning is a little tricky to explain but, as simply as we can put it, the meaning is to communicate that you see… And the word is **ZYXT**!

# Infinite Monkeys and Endless Gratitude

The Infinite Monkey Theorem proposes that, if you give an infinite number of monkeys an infinite number of typewriters, and an infinite amount of time, they will eventually recreate the entire works of Shakespeare. Quite what would motivate an infinite number of monkeys to sit down and start typing away in the first place is not at all clear to us…

However, despite producing this book using significantly fewer typewriters, and comparatively little time, we now believe that those monkeys won't be able to do it alone. They'll need help[†]... That being the case, any Infinite Monkey Project would benefit from enlisting the following people, to whom we express our own great appreciation: Rena Nathanson and her children, Aaron & Ava; the BANANAGRAMS Bunch; Lesley Singleton; Stu Turner; Gary Bensley; Charly Sommers; Vaila Donnachie; Abigael Crowe; Byron Schmuland; The Globe Theatre London; W.C. Minor, Crowthorne, Berkshire; and to Chloe Flexman, without whom all is chaos.

This book is dedicated to Abe & Sandy Nathanson, Nancy & John Johnson and to all parents that have infinite patience for their monkeys... And to the monkeys that subsequently express their endless gratitude!

---

[†]We wrote to some monkeys asking for a comment on the subject; they released the following statement: jjhduh{rvagdu@gfgukefh#$uwevu/ weiygwqsjopqoj{{"upcfpsopuupcf,uibujtuifrvftujpo..."

# Index

# Collins

## LITTLE BOOKS

These beautifully presented Little Books make excellent pocket-sized guides, packed with hints and tips.

**101 ways to win at Scrabble**
978-0-00-758914-2
£6.99

**Bridge Secrets**
978-0-00-825047-8
£6.99

**Gin**
978-0-00-825810-8
£6.99

**Whisky**
978-0-00-825108-6
£6.99

**Scottish Castles**
978-0-00-825111-6
£6.99

**Scottish Dance**
978-0-00-821056-4
£6.99

**Scottish History**
978-0-00-825110-9
£6.99

**Clans and Tartans**
978-0-00-825109-3
£6.99

Available to buy from all good booksellers and online.
All titles are also available as ebooks.
**www.collins.co.uk**

 @collins_ref      facebook.com/collinsref

# HarperCollins
## PUBLISHERS
*Since 1817*